SpringerBriefs in Psychology

SpringerBriefs in School Psychology

More information about this series at http://www.springer.com/series/10143

Hala Mohammed Berri • Anies Al-Hroub

ADHD in Lebanese Schools

Diagnosis, Assessment, and Treatment

Springer

Hala Mohammed Berri
Department of Education
American University of Beirut
Beirut, Lebanon

Anies Al-Hroub
Department of Education
American University of Beirut
Beirut, Lebanon

ISSN 2192-8363 ISSN 2192-8371 (electronic)
SpringerBriefs in Psychology
ISBN 978-3-319-28698-3 ISBN 978-3-319-28700-3 (eBook)
DOI 10.1007/978-3-319-28700-3

Library of Congress Control Number: 2016931325

Springer Cham Heidelberg New York Dordrecht London

Printed on acid-free paper

Springer International Publishing AG Switzerland is part of Springer Science+Business Media (www.springer.com)

For my parents and family

Hala Mohamad Berri

For all my graduate students

Anies Al-Hroub

Preface

This new book brings together the latest research about attention deficit hyperactivity disorder (ADHD) in Lebanon. It specifically addresses issues related to assessing, diagnosing, and treating students with ADHD in Lebanese schools. The book is primarily written for teachers, counselors, principals, and researchers. It also addresses specialists who are working with children with ADHD and special educational needs.

The structure of chapters addresses what teachers and practitioners should do when dealing with issues related to ADHD. Chapter 1 introduces the concept of ADHD and the types of difficulty which children with the disorder experience at school. The aims, rationale, and significance of the research study on which this book is based are outlined. In Chap. 2 we discuss how the concept of ADHD has evolved over time and then move on to an examination of the prevalence, causes, diagnosis, and treatment of the disorder. In addition, we look at teachers' knowledge and perceptions of ADHD. We then describe in Chap. 3 the research study that we undertook and how we set about answering our two research questions, which aimed to investigate Lebanese elementary school teachers' knowledge of ADHD and how the gender of students with the disorder affects teachers' perceptions of ADHD subtypes. The research findings are presented in Chap. 4, and we discuss teachers' general knowledge about ADHD as well as their understanding of the symptoms, diagnosis, and treatment of the condition. In addition we provide an overview of ADHD in the specific context of Lebanon. Chapter 5 concludes the book with a discussion of what constitutes teacher's knowledge and perceptions of ADHD and the need for training to be provided for teachers and services to be offered to students. We consider the implications of the research and make recommendations for strategies that will benefit both students and teachers alike.

Beirut, Lebanon

Hala Mohammed Berri
Anies Al-Hroub

Contents

Abbreviations

AAP	American Academy of Pediatrics
ADD	Attention Deficit Disorder
ADHD	Attention Deficit Hyperactivity Disorder
APA	American Psychological Association
ASCA	American School Counselor Association
AUB	American University of Beirut
CFTMEA	Classification Française des Troubles Mentaux de l'Enfant Et de l'Adolescent
DSM	Diagnostic and Statistical Manual of Mental Disorder
DSM III	Diagnostic and Statistical Manual of Mental Disorders, 3rd Edition
DSM III—R	Diagnostic and Statistical Manual of Mental Disorders, Third Edition, Revised
DSM IV	Diagnostic and Statistical Manual of Mental Disorders, 4th Edition
DSM IV—TR	Diagnostic and Statistical Manual of Mental Disorders, 4th Edition, Text Revision
DSM V	Diagnostic and Statistical Manual of Mental Disorders, 5th Edition
FGD	Focus Group Discussion
IRB	Institutional Review Board
KADDS	Knowledge of Attention Deficit Disorders Scale
MEHE	Ministry of Education and Higher Education
MENA	Middle East and North Africa
SPSS	Statistical Package for the Social Science

List of Figure

List of Tables

About the Authors

Hala Mohammed Berri is the educational coordinator of NASMA Learning and Resource Centre, working with Syrian refugees and underprivileged children from different areas of Beirut. Ms. Berri completed her MA in educational psychology (with emphasis on school guidance and counseling), BA in elementary education (with emphasis on math and science education), and teaching diploma in special education from the American University of Beirut (AUB). She led a number of educational projects and workshops sponsored by ARAMEX tackling the Syrians' crises and participated in many conferences about child protection in Lebanon.

Anies Al-Hroub is the chairperson of the Department of Education at the American University of Beirut. He is an associate professor of education psychology and special education and the coordinator of the special education program. Al-Hroub completed his PhD and MPhil in special education (giftedness and learning disabilities) from the University of Cambridge and his MA (special education) and BA (psychology) from the University of Jordan. He also obtained a higher diploma in "learning disabilities" from Balka Applied University. He was selected as the British Academy visiting scholar to the Faculty of Education at the University of Cambridge in 2010. His publications appeared in leading international gifted and special education journals in addition to a book published titled *Theories and Programs of Education for the Gifted and Talented*. Al-Hroub's research interests focus on gifted and talented education, learning disabilities, dyslexia, dual exceptionality, early childhood education, educational assessment, psychometric and dynamic assessment, guidance and counseling, metacognition, and school dropout. He led a number of educational projects sponsored by UNICEF, UNRWA, the British Academy, USAID, Issam Fares Institute for Public Policy and International Affairs (IFI), and Welfare Association and served as consultant for UNESCO and the Center for Civic Engagement and Community Service (CCECS) at AUB.

Chapter 1
Introduction to ADHD

1.1 Introduction

The concept of attention deficit hyperactivity disorder (ADHD) has evolved gradually and still carries some traces of its origins. Historically, two extreme points of view have been dominant (Taylor, 2011). One describes ADHD as a biological condition of the brain, resulting from genetics and the physical environment, while the other extreme describes ADHD as a psychological variant rather than a disorder, with problems deriving from societal intolerance or from the need for supportive and educational measures (Taylor, 2011). Today, ADHD is characterized as a developmental, neurobiological condition defined by the presence of severe and pervasive symptoms of inattention, hyperactivity, and impulsivity (Daley & Birchwood, 2010). It is becoming one of the most prevalent childhood and adolescence disorders, affecting from 5 to 10 % of all US school-age children (ASCA, 2012).

Given the high incidence of ADHD in school populations, teachers are likely to teach multiple children with ADHD (Legato, 2011). These children have difficulty waiting their turn, talk excessively, often appear not to be listening when being spoken to, and tend to interrupt and intrude on others in games, conversations, and classroom discussions (Daley & Birchwood, 2010). Those who exhibit such behavioral problems in the classroom, whether displaying symptoms of inattention and/or hyperactivity, are at higher risk of poor scholastic achievement and dropping out of school (Martinussen, Tannock, & Chaban, 2011). According to the American School Counselor Association (ASCA, 2012), ADHD may severely affect family relations, cause problems with school staff, impede learning and academic achievement, interfere with peer relationships, and contribute to a student's poor self-concept and low self-esteem. Since ADHD is a disorder that takes place within the school setting either in the classroom and has undesirable effects in terms of academic achievement of students, teachers are often in the front line when it comes to identifying the condition and helping students who suffer from it (Badeleh, 2013). Teachers need to be aware of the symptoms of ADHD in order to be able to identify

H.M. Berri, A. Al-Hroub, *ADHD in Lebanese Schools*,
Springer Briefs in Psychology, DOI 10.1007/978-3-319-28700-3_1

students affected by it and refer them for help. Before any intervention or treatment, a correct diagnosis should be made (Krowski, 2009).

From another perspective, teachers' perceptions of ADHD children may differ according to the child's gender (Maniadaki, Sonuga-Barke, & Kakouros, 2003). Given the importance of (a) the interactions between these children and their teachers and (b) early identification, the impact of the ADHD students' gender on teachers' perceptions may be considered an important factor (Maniadaki et al., 2003). Research indicates that there are about 2.5 boys for every girl with ADHD and about six boys for every girl with ADHD referred to clinics in the USA (Ohan & Visser, 2009). A similar discrepancy based on gender has also been identified in Australia. This gender discrepancy emphasizes the potential problems that can influence diagnosis of students with ADHD and the role that teachers play in identifying the condition; this is because teachers have different expectations of, and behave differently toward, boys and girls (Ohan & Visser, 2009). Boys with ADHD typically exhibit high levels of hyperactivity, aggressiveness, and other externalizing symptoms, which teachers perceive to be disruptive and stressful (Sciutto, Nolfi, & Bluhm, 2004). Girls with ADHD, however, tend to exhibit lower levels of disruptive behavior but higher levels of inattentiveness, internalizing symptoms, and social impairment (Sciutto et al., 2004). Girls with ADHD are considerably under-recognized by teachers and under-referred when compared with boys affected by the condition (Groenewald, Emond, & Sayal, 2009). Alarmingly, some studies estimate that as many as 50–70 % of girls with ADHD fail to be diagnosed (Adams, 2007). A major reason is that bias in teachers' perceptions of boys' and girls' behaviors contributes to gender differences in relation to ADHD referrals (Sciutto et al., 2004). Girls with ADHD are less likely to be referred because they cause fewer problems in the classroom, while boys' symptoms of impulsiveness and hyperactivity are more likely to be noted by teachers (Adams, 2007). Teacher bias may also be the result of their lack of knowledge of ADHD subtypes (Bauermeister et al., 2007), and international research has shown the difficulties teachers have in recognizing girls with ADHD (Groenewald et al., 2009). It is clear that teachers play an important role in the recognition and referral of children with ADHD (Groenewald et al., 2009). They are often seen as the most valuable source of information about a child's behavior, and any bias in teacher perceptions may have important consequences for the child and the school (Sciutto et al., 2004). No studies have been found that have been conducted in the context of Arab countries. In sum, it is very important to investigate the effects of a child's gender and ADHD types on teachers' perceptions and referral decisions.

In the research study reported here, a demographic questionnaire was administered with teachers to obtain information about their age, gender, and teaching experience (e.g., length of teaching experience, grades taught, etc.). The knowledge of attention deficit disorder scale (KADDS) was then used to measure teachers' knowledge of the symptoms, associated features, and treatment of ADHD. Four vignettes that describe a boy with ADHD, a girl with ADHD, a boy with attention deficit disorder (ADD), and a girl with ADD were then used to gauge the extent to which teachers differ in their perceptions according to gender difference and ADHD types. Finally, focus-group discussions took place in order to enable the researcher to obtain in-depth understanding of teachers' perceptions and understanding of ADHD.

1.2 Discovering What Lebanese Teachers Know About ADHD

The aim of this study was twofold: (a) to explore elementary teachers' current knowledge and ADHD in Lebanon; and (b) to investigate the nature of the relationship between ADHD and students' gender and its implications for teachers' perceptions of ADHD subtypes. Two questions guided the current research study:

1. What knowledge do Lebanese teachers in the elementary cycle have about ADHD?
2. How does ADHD students' gender affect elementary teachers' perceptions of ADHD subtypes?

1.3 Why Study ADHD in Lebanon?

There is a lack of theoretical and empirical studies on school guidance and counseling in the context of the Middle East and North Africa (MENA) region. Moreover, knowledge about students' needs and the tasks of counselors and teachers in this regard requires further development. Studies conducted in the region, for example, Turkey and Iran, have found that teachers lack knowledge about ADHD. In Turkey, for example, 65.5 % of teachers believed that ADHD is a consequence of parental spoiling according to Nur and Kavakci (2010). Another study carried out in Isfahan, Iran, showed that teachers had little knowledge of ADHD, and they were in genuine need of workshops and training in order to enhance their knowledge about how to deal with ADHD students (Sarraf, Karahmadi, Marasy, & Azhar, 2011). Moreover, published studies in the Arab world are also scarce (Farah et al., 2009). The researcher examined the MA theses that had been conducted in the Lebanese context and did found that these studies focused on ADHD children rather than on teachers and did so from an interventionist aspect. They basically targeted the effect of training on such students, how to include them in a general education setting, and the different interventions that would help teachers deal with them. However, none of these studies has ascertained whether teachers are knowledgeable about ADHD symptoms, the possible overlaps and confusions between ADHD/ADD, and other behavioral problems, such as aggression in males and quietness and restlessness in females.

According to the ASCA (2012), school counselors should uphold the rights of students with ADHD to receive multidisciplinary, multimodal, and multifaceted treatment for symptoms and effects of ADHD. Ayyash-Abdo, Alamuddin, and Mukallid (2010) believe that school counseling in Lebanon is in need of development, especially in southern Lebanon. This viewpoint reflects the reality in Lebanon that ADHD has been almost entirely ignored in both practice and area for research. This is an immediate cause for concern with regard to students who display ADHD in schools and their teachers' ability to identify and cope with these students.

Previous research in Western cultures has found evidence that teachers lack knowledge about ADHD and that they require comprehensive training to help them deal with children who have the condition (Nur & Kavakci, 2010). Other research studies have adapted the KADDS to measure teachers' knowledge of the symptoms, associated features, and treatment of ADHD. It has been found that KADDS scores are positively related to teachers' prior knowledge, attitudes, and self-efficacy (Sciutto et al., 2004). Therefore, our own study is founded on previous studies that have been carried out in different Western cultures, and we hope that as a result of our research, the term "teachers' knowledge" will subsequently be used in the Lebanese literature as it is a prerequisite for the intervention studies that other researchers have already conducted.

On another level, most teachers in our Arab culture lack knowledge about ADHD and may fail to understand its symptoms (Farah et al., 2009). A study done in Australia has shown that girls are less likely to be identified as children with ADHD due to the fact that they receive less attention from teachers (Ohan & Visser, 2009). ADD girls are considered to be more at risk and of greater concern than boys as they are more likely to suffer from emotional problems, such as depression, anxiety, and loneliness (Maniadaki et al., 2003). Another study conducted in England has shown that ADHD in girls as compared with the disorder in boys is under-recognized and that teachers have difficulty in coping with, and have poor knowledge of, ADHD subtypes (Groenewald et al., 2009). Therefore, improving teachers' knowledge about ADHD, in relation to inattention, could assist in tackling gender gaps and bias when it comes to requesting referrals and accurate diagnosis. Moreover, sociocultural expectations of boys' and girls' behavior differ (Maniadaki et al., 2003). In most Arab societies, quietness, fearfulness, and dependency are considered normal for girls, whereas aggression and impulsiveness are regarded as traits which are typical of boys. On the basis of their personal experience of teaching, teachers immediately label boys who show disruptive behaviors in the classroom as aggressive and hyperactive without taking account of the difference between aggression and hyperactivity. Moreover, teachers neglect girls due to their quietness, ignoring the fact that ADHD can appear in other subtypes like ADD. Further explanation of ADHD subtypes is provided in Chap. 2.

Our choice of topic for this study stemmed from the fact that teachers' knowledge about ADHD in Lebanon, specifically in southern Lebanon, is poorly developed, and this needs to be examined thoroughly by investigating the level of awareness that teachers have of ADHD and how gender bias affects their response to it. Are there differences in the way they respond to boys and girls? Without adequate knowledge or training on how to address the needs of ADHD children in the classroom, teachers may feel unprepared to face many challenges that such children can present, and they may be less likely to seek appropriate support for their students (Legato, 2011). Therefore, improving teachers' knowledge about ADHD is essential if they are able to identify these students with ADHD from others and, thus, adopt good pre-intervention techniques.

1.4 Addressing the Difficulties in Educating Students with ADHD

Our study aims to have an impact on both the theory of counseling and the practice of working with ADHD students. Theoretically speaking, identifying the knowledge that teachers possess about ADHD is a prerequisite for any future study intending to initiate intervention programs. Moreover, the results of this study will be of use in producing a more comprehensive definition of ADHD, taking into account possible cultural biases that affect the understanding of the condition. Comprehensive programs cannot exist if the concept of ADHD is unclear.

At a practical level, identifying Lebanese elementary school teachers' knowledge about ADHD and its relationship to gender differences will help educators to explore and address the deficiencies of the educational system. This will help teachers and practitioners to prepare appropriate in-service training programs and workshops. Teachers can play a major role in recognizing, identifying, and referring students. Therefore, teachers' workshops accompanied by comprehensive school guidance and curriculum programs would be a first step toward progress.

References

Adams, C. (2007). Girls & ADHD: Are you missing the signs? *Instructor, 116*, 31–35.

American School Counselor Association. (2012). *ASCA national model A framwork for school counseling programs*. Retrieved from http://schoolcounselor.org/ascanationalmodel/media/anm-templates/anmexecsumm.pdf

Ayyash-Abdo, H., Alamuddin, R., & Mukallid, S. (2010). School counseling in Lebanon: Past, present, and future. *Journal of Counseling & Development, 88*, 13–17.

Badeleh, M. T. (2013). Attention deficit hyperactivity disorder and elementary teachers' awareness. *Journal of Medical Sciences, 13*, 829–833.

Bauermeister, J. J., Shrout, P. E., Chávez, L., Rubio-Stipec, M., Ramírez, R., Padilla, L., Anderson, A., García, P., Canino, G. (2007). ADHD and gender: Are risks and sequela of ADHD the same for boys and girls? *Journal of Child Psychology and Psychiatry, and Allied Disciplines, 48*, 831–839.

Daley, D., & Birchwood, J. (2010). ADHD and academic performance: Why does ADHD impact on academic performance and what can be done to support ADHD children in the classroom?: ADHD and academic performance. *Child: Care, Health and Development, 36*, 455–464.

Farah, L. G., Fayyad, J. A., Eapen, V., Cassir, Y., Salamoun, M. M., Tabet, C. C., et al. (2009). ADHD in the Arab world a review of epidemiologic studies. *Journal of Attention Disorders, 13*, 211–222.

Groenewald, C., Emond, A., & Sayal, K. (2009). Recognition and referral of girls with attention deficit hyperactivity disorder: Case vignette study. *Child: Care, Health and Development, 35*, 767–772.

Krowski, K. F. (2009). ADHD: *Urban teachers' knowledge, beliefs and classroom practice*. University of Massachusetts. Theses and Dissertations. Retrieved from http://search.proquest.com/docview/305140059?accountid=8555

Legato, J. (2011). *Effects of teacher factors on expectations of students with ADHD*. DePaul University. Theses and Dissertations. Retrieved from http://via.library.depaul.edu/etd/66

Maniadaki, K., Sonuga-Barke, E. J. S., & Kakouros, E. (2003). Trainee nursery teachers' perceptions of disruptive behaviour disorders; the effect of sex of child on judgments of typicality and severity. *Child: Care, Health and Development, 29*, 433–440.

Martinussen, R., Tannock, R., & Chaban, P. (2011). Teachers' reported use of instructional and behavior management practices for students with behavior problems: Relationship to role and level of training in ADHD. *Child & Youth Care Forum, 40*, 193–210.

Nur, N., & Kavakci, O. (2010). Elementary school teachers' knowledge and attitudes related to attention deficit hyperactivity disorder. *Journal of Society for Development in New Net Environment in B&H, 4*, 350–355.

Ohan, J. L., & Visser, T. A. (2009). Why is there a gender gap in children presenting for attention deficit/hyperactivity disorder services? *Journal of Clinical Child and Adolescent Psychology, 38*, 650–660.

Sarraf, N., Karahmadi, M., Marasy, M. R., & Azhar, S. M. (2011). A comparative study of the effectiveness of nonattendance and workshop education of primary school teachers in their knowledge, attitude and function towards ADHD students in Isfahan in 2010. *Journal of Research in Medical Sciences, 16*, 1196–1201.

Sciutto, M. J., Nolfi, C. J., & Bluhm, C. (2004). Effects of child gender and symptom type on referrals for ADHD by elementary school teachers. *Journal of Emotional and Behavioral Disorders, 12*, 247–253.

Taylor, E. (2011). Antecedents of ADHD: A historical account of diagnostic concepts. *Attention Deficit and Hyperactivity Disorders, 3*, 69–75.

Chapter 2
Assessment, Diagnosis, and Treatment of ADHD in School-Aged Children

2.1 Conceptions of ADHD

2.1.1 Evolving Conceptions of ADHD

ADHD, the abbreviation for attention deficit hyperactivity disorder, is used to describe children, adolescents, and some adults, who show hyperactive, impulsive, and/or markedly inattentive behavior (Kleynhans, 2005). Under different names, ADHD has been recognized for more than a century. In the nineteenth century, Heinrich Hoffman (1809–1894), a German physician and poet, wrote about Fidgety Philip who could not keep still. He often creates a mess and upsets his parents (Taylor, 2011). The poem portrays the typical behavior of a child with ADHD, living in times when children were subject to more severe forms of discipline than they are today (Millichap, 2010).

In the early twentieth century, George Frederick Still, the founder of pediatrics in England, described ADHD with a modern understanding of the condition (Taylor, 2011). His descriptions of problem behavior certainly overlap with ADHD but do not, however, give primacy to impulsiveness, overactivity, or inattention (Taylor, 2011). Rather he aims to describe it as "defects of moral control" and attributes behavior problems to constitutional medical conditions (Taylor, 2011).

Medical references to childhood behavioral problems date back to the beginning of the twentieth century. Behavioral abnormalities were associated with head injury, and they also occurred as a complication of encephalitis following the influenza epidemic of 1918 (Millichap, 2010). This condition was first observed in Vienna, in soldiers who had survived World War I. It affected all ages and produced a variety of neurological symptoms, with sometimes excited overactivity, involuntary movements, sleep disorders, mood changes, and manic behavior (Taylor, 2011). This contributed to what we would now refer to as ADHD.

The next step was, therefore, to move to a definition based on psychological changes rather than unknowable neurological ones (Taylor, 2011). Two American

H.M. Berri, A. Al-Hroub, *ADHD in Lebanese Schools*,
Springer Briefs in Psychology, DOI 10.1007/978-3-319-28700-3_2

authors made further contributions: Virginia Douglas proposed the concept of attention deficit and Paul Wender regarded attention deficits as the key to understanding minimal brain damage (MBD) (Taylor, 2011). The stage was set for the development of the key idea of attention deficit disorder, which appeared in the third edition of the Diagnostic and Statistical Manual of the American Psychiatric Association (Taylor, 2011). At this point, the early era of the understanding of ADHD came to a close.

2.1.2 Current Definition of ADHD

The initial descriptions of brain damage syndrome in children with brain injuries progressed to the point when minimal brain damage was defined, after which the emphasis turned to symptoms, with the American Psychiatric Association including the syndrome in their Diagnostic and Statistical Manual (DSM) in 1968 (Millichap, 2010). ADHD was originally presented in the DSM-II as a disorder involving hyperactivity. The inattention subtype was not formally recognized until 1980 (Bell, 2013), when the DSM-III recognized two subtypes in the syndrome of attention deficit disorder (ADD): ADD with hyperactivity and ADD without hyperactivity. In 1987, the DSM-III was revised (DSM-III-R), and the term attention deficit hyperactivity disorder (ADHD) was used. In 1994, the DSM-IV recognized three subtypes of the syndrome: ADHD-inattentive type, ADHD-hyperactive-impulsive type, and ADHD-combined type (Millichap, 2010). Finally, with the publication of the DSM-V in 2013, a more accurate characterization of the experience of affected adults was presented (APA, 2013). By adapting the criteria for adults, DSM-V aims to ensure that children with ADHD can continue to receive care throughout their lives if needed (APA, 2013).

2.2 Overview of ADHD

2.2.1 Prevalence of ADHD and Gender Factors

The prevalence of ADHD varies across cultures. Its reported prevalence in school-age children varies from 2 to 18 % according to the diagnostic criteria listed in DSM-IV (Alloway, Elliott, & Holmes, 2010). Boys are affected three to six times more commonly than girls (Millichap, 2010).

The condition affects millions of children around the world. Approximately 3–5 % of elementary school children in the USA have been diagnosed with this disorder (Kleynhans, 2005). In the UK, a study was conducted to explore the prevalence of ADHD symptoms in a community sample of 964 10-year-old children (Alloway et al., 2010). Results showed the existence of ADHD in 8 % of the sample, with the majority of those children being boys who were identified with the hyperactive/impulsive subtype (Alloway et al., 2010). A study investigating the prevalence of this disorder in 1658 students in the Middle East, particularly in Tabriz, Iran, showed similar results (Amiri, Fakhari, Maheri, & Asl, 2010). The prevalence rate of ADHD in these elementary students in Tabriz was 9.7 %, and the disorder was more common among boys (Amiri et al., 2010). Boys are more frequently referred than girls, with estimates ranging from 6 to 9 % of boys and 2–3 % of girls in schools (Kleynhans, 2005).

The high prevalence of ADHD can result in undesirable effects on the academic achievement of students (Badeleh, 2013). Thus, teachers are expected to play a major role in helping these students and in preventing the complications that may arise from this disorder (Badeleh, 2013).

2.2.2 Prevalence of ADHD Across Cultures

Cultural differences in the diagnosis and treatment of ADHD are important issues to be considered because they are influenced to a great extent by the background culture of the family and teachers' perceptions (AAP, 2011). Variations in the reported prevalence of ADHD depend on the diagnostic criteria that each country uses (Krowski, 2009). The DSM-IV is frequently used in the USA, and Europeans have developed their own guidelines for diagnosing hyperkinetic disorder in accordance with the DSM-IV (Graham, Seth, & Coghill, 2007). However, the French do not use the same system as the one used by American psychiatrists (Wedge, 2012). The French Federation of Psychiatry has developed the CFTMEA (Classification Francaise des Troubles Mentaux de L'Enfant et de L'Adolescent), the focus of which is on identifying and addressing the causes of the symptoms experienced by children with ADHD (Wedge, 2012). Taking into account the different tools and guidelines used for diagnosing children with ADHD, prevalence among these countries varies. ADHD remains higher in the USA (8 %) where the DSM-IV is used, while it remains underdiagnosed in France and Europe (4–5 %) (Krowski, 2009).

2.2.3 Causes of ADHD

The possible causes of ADHD are heritability, antenatal environment, and home and social environment.

With regard to heritability, high levels have been found in relation to ADHD, and the disorder does appear to run in families (Howe, 2010). One study has found that neurological and genetic factors are the greatest contributors to this disorder (Kleynhans, 2005). Many genes are likely to be involved, but those related to dopamine neurotransmission and serotonin pathways in the brain have been strongly implicated (Howe, 2010). Due to the fact that ADHD is a familial disorder, it is possible that when a child is diagnosed with ADHD, either one or both parents may also suffer from the disorder (Kleynhans, 2005). This fact has implications for teachers in terms of their communication with parents and their need to develop a deeper understanding of the child (Kleynhans, 2005).

Neurological studies have suggested that the prefrontal cortex, part of the cerebellum, and the basal ganglia may be involved in the symptoms of ADHD. They may cause inattention and problems with inhibition (Kleynhans, 2005). A number of antenatal environmental risk factors with respect to ADHD have also been suggested. Tobacco smoking, alcohol consumption by the mother during pregnancy, prenatal maternal stress, prematurity, and low birth weight have been identified as possible risk factors (Howe, 2010).

As far as home and social environment are concerned, inadequate parental discipline has been suggested as one of the factors that could lead to greater severity in symptoms (Howe, 2010). Many comorbid disorders may associate with ADHD, such as conduct disorders, depression, and anxiety (Pires, da Silva, & de Assis, 2013). A study conducted in São Gonçalo, Brazil, sought to ascertain whether family and environmental factors are associated with the appearance of ADHD in children (Pires et al., 2013). Results showed that more severe symptoms in the children were associated with higher levels of family dysfunction (Pires et al., 2013). Sixty-two percent of the clinicians said that they had assessed the family situation and parenting factors and believed that presumed environmental "causes" such as negative school experiences, relationship problems, a chaotic family background, or a history of child abuse or neglect may lead to a greater severity of ADHD symptoms (Kovshoff et al., 2012).

2.2.4 Genetic and/or Psychosocial Causes of ADHD

The causes of ADHD are still a matter for debate in the UK in terms of medical and biological explanations (Salway, 2010). Two have been identified: the first (biological) depicts ADHD as a brain disorder of genetic origin, which is treated as a medical condition, and the second (psychosocial) considers ADHD to be the consequence of poor parenting, school discipline, and associated with the general state of society (Salway, 2010). The psychosocial set of explanations is overwhelmingly dominant in the UK, and parents of ADHD children are blamed because they work long hours, which places a strain on family life. As a result, their children are victims of parental work conditions. Moreover, parents are also represented as ineffective, seeking excuses for their children's inappropriate behavior (Salway, 2010). The French also view ADHD as a medical condition that has psychosocial and situational causes (Wedge, 2012), with French doctors preferring to look at the child's social context and not at the child's brain. This is very different from the American tendency to attribute symptoms to a biological dysfunction, such as a chemical imbalance in the child's brain (Wedge, 2012). Moreover, according to Wedge (2012), parenting styles differ between cultures. French parents provide their children with a firm structure and clear discipline. Children are not allowed, for example, to have a snack whenever they want one; mealtimes are at four specific times of the day so French children learn to wait patiently for their meal rather than eating whenever they want. Furthermore, parents are consistent with their rules and discipline as they believe that these will make their children feel safer and will result in better behavior (Wedge, 2012). In South Korea, the traditional culture of Confucianism is a strong influence on parenting practices, and obedience is an essential value that influences family harmony and functioning. The disruptive behavior of ADHD children can be seen as a dishonor to a family and is often viewed pejoratively by others in Korean society (Oh, Park, Suk, Song, & Im, 2012). Unfortunately, this very strict parenting style affects children with ADHD negatively. According to Oh et al. (2012), authoritarian parenting practices are associated with poor social adjustment skills and more anxiety and aggression in children. An affectionate parenting attitude is important in preventing behavioral problems in ADHD children.

Research in cultures such as those of the Near East, particularly in Turkey and Iran, view ADHD as a result of the environment, regarding parental spoiling as the main cause (Ghanizadeh, Bahredar, & Moeini, 2005; Nur & Kavakci, 2010). Another study, conducted by Maniadaki, Sonuga-Barke, and Kakouros (2003), highlights ADHD students' gender as a possible cultural factor influencing teachers' referrals. As mentioned in previous sections, teachers' referrals are subject to their preferences and to cultural expectations of boys and girls as well.

Thus, on the basis of the research findings discussed above, it is clear that teachers' and parents' perspectives on ADHD are influenced by culture, the role of which is very important. In Korea, in accordance with Confucianism, parents and teachers tend to focus more on children's academic achievement and regard children's disruptive behavior as a negative reflection on themselves and their authority. They generally take personal responsibility for such behavior problems on the part of their children and have negative attitudes toward medication because it does not help to enhance academic achievement (Moon, 2011). US parents and teachers, influenced by Western culture's focus on independence, tend not to take personal responsibility for the children's behavior but focus more on children's current problems and treatment. These parents and teachers are happy to accept a third party's engagement in dealing with children with ADHD and their behavior. US parents are more positive about medical treatment because medication helps to reduce children's disruptive behavior (Moon, 2011). Clearly, different perspectives on ADHD exist and these are strongly influenced by culture.

2.2.5 Diagnosis of ADHD

A diagnosis of ADHD is essential to providing help for students with ADHD. It is performed by psychologists or clinicians, most of whom stress the important role that parents and teachers play in this process. Some clinicians speak of teachers as the more experienced judges of typical and atypical behavior based on their experience with multiple children in different settings (Kovshoff et al., 2012). Kovshoff et al. (2012) report that teachers are accorded greater trust than parents since they spend more time with children. In addition, teachers have broad experience as a result of dealing with many different children. Finally, in a large class of students, the teacher can easily identify any abnormal behavior.

Extensive research has found that the primary symptoms displayed by ADHD children are inattention, impulsiveness, and hyperactivity (Barkley, 2005). With regard to inattention, children with ADHD have difficulty sustaining attention when doing independent school homework or carrying out tasks that are dull or boring for them (Barkley, 2005). Impulsiveness in children with ADHD is demonstrated by their difficulty in inhibiting and self-regulating their behavior (Barkley, 2005). Finally, when it comes to hyperactivity, children with ADHD are extremely active and energetic, often moving around without permission, talking excessively, and leaving their seats (Barkley, 2005).

Most professionals base their diagnosis of ADHD on the guidelines of the American Psychiatric Association's Diagnostic and Statistical Manual of Mental disorders (Kleynhans, 2005). Teachers are expected to be aware of the main symptoms and subtypes of ADHD. However, these diagnostic criteria could also be of benefit when making an appropriate referral.

2.2.6 Assessment of ADHD

The purpose of assessment is to determine whether or not a child should be diagnosed with ADHD in the absence or presence of other childhood psychiatric disorders: this of course requires extensive clinical knowledge of such disorders. Another purpose of assessment is to address the academic and social problems that have been noticed through the use of appropriate intervention plans (Kleynhans, 2005).

Following a teacher's referral of a child showing ADHD-related symptoms, the first stage of assessment is to obtain the teacher's ratings of the child's behavior. If it becomes evident during the first stage that there are significant problems, then the assessment process moves on to the second stage, during which multiple assessment methods are used. The psychologist then intervenes and interviews the child, the parents, and the teacher in order to prepare an intervention and treatment plan. During the third phase of assessment, the results of the multi-method evaluation are interpreted. Finally, an intervention and treatment plan is devised during the fourth stage of the assessment (Kleynhans, 2005).

Teachers spend most of their time with students, whether in the classroom or during free time, and thus, they play a major role in referring children for assessment. They are expected to complete behavior-rating scales after referring a child and are the source of detailed information about the referred child required by the psychologist. Such information includes the referred child's academic performance, social relations, the difficulties that the child faces, and the strategies that the teacher uses to address such difficulties. Teachers also need to review the DSM-IV diagnostic criteria with the psychologist in order to match their own observations with such criteria (Kleynhans, 2005). Teachers' collaboration with parents and specialists is fundamental to the success of the assessment process so that good referrals and accurate diagnosis may be made.

2.2.7 *Intervention and Treatment*

To date, evidence-based research on treatments for ADHD has centered on medication and behavioral interventions (Krowski, 2009). There are three types of medication: stimulants, antidepressants, and antihypertensives (Barkley & Mash, 2006). Medication was highly recommended for ADHD children by 60 % of the teachers in Gregg's (2005) study. Based on interviews and questionnaires completed by elementary teachers, results showed that most teachers viewed medication as a type of intervention that could provide a short-term reduction in inappropriate behavior (Gregg, 2005). However, Morisoli and McLaughlin (2006) believe that behavioral interventions have a greater impact on ADHD children. In their study, based on 350 teachers in Wisconsin and Minnesota, 78 % of these teachers pointed out that medication do not obviate the need for effective interventions that aim to improve learning and achievement (Morisoli & McLaughlin, 2006). A combination of both stimulant medication and behavioral interventions produces far better results in children with ADHD than medication alone.

2.3 Teachers' Knowledge of ADHD

Teachers' knowledge about how to deal with ADHD plays a major role in improving the academic and social functioning of children with the disorder (Barkley, 2005). It has been shown that teachers who have poor knowledge and understanding of ADHD tend to have a negative impact on these students (Barkley, 2005). One study conducted in Korea aimed to understand the perspectives of teachers who taught children with ADHD (Hong, 2008). Twenty-seven teachers at a Seoul school completed a short survey in which they wrote narrative descriptions of their thoughts about ADHD, and the findings indicated that they lacked knowledge about ADHD and faced problems in distinguishing ADHD symptoms from those of other disorders (Hong, 2008). In a different context, a quantitative study examined the levels of knowledge about ADHD of 107 school teachers in South Texas (Guerra & Brown, 2012). The study specifically compared teachers' levels of knowledge in relation to three specific areas: (a) general knowledge of ADHD, (b) knowledge of symptoms and diagnosis of ADHD, and (c) knowledge of treatments for ADHD (Guerra & Brown, 2012). The three subscales were measured using the study instrument, knowledge of attention deficit disorders scale (KADDS). The data analysis indicated that the levels of knowledge of ADHD among middle school teachers in South Texas were low, with scale knowledge scores ranging from 46 to 66 %; general knowledge had the lowest score in the study sample (Guerra & Brown, 2012).

Weyandt, Fulton, Schepman, Verdi, and Wilson (2009) investigated the level of knowledge about ADHD in a sample of 130 general education teachers, special education teachers, and school psychologists who responded to a 24-item questionnaire concerning possible causes of, and treatment for, ADHD (Weyandt et al., 2009). Findings revealed that the school psychologists' level of knowledge of ADHD was significantly greater than that of special and general education teachers. However, there were no significant differences between the level of knowledge of general education teachers and their special education counterparts in relation to ADHD. In both groups, accurate knowledge was limited. In examining the false beliefs that existed among the participants in the study, general education teachers and special education teachers proved to be those who agreed most often with the statement, "Special diets are effective treatments for ADHD," a widely accepted myth that frequently emerged (Weyandt et al., 2009).

Nur and Kavakci (2010) conducted a study in Turkey of elementary teachers from 87 schools to explore their knowledge about ADHD. The findings of the study showed that teachers' knowledge was insufficient: 88 % of teachers rated their own levels of information about ADHD as very low and 65.5 % of teachers believed that the disorder was a consequence of parental spoiling. In addition, television, advice from friends, and articles in newspapers were identified by teachers as their main sources of information about ADHD (Nur & Kavakci, 2010). Similarly, the findings of the study by Ghanizadeh et al. (2005) concurred with those of previous research studies, demonstrating that 53 % of Iranian teachers considered ADHD to be the result of parental spoiling (Ghanizadeh et al., 2005). An Australian study grouped two samples of teachers into categories indicating high or low levels of knowledge about ADHD in accordance with their responses to an ADHD survey (Legato, 2011). This study indicated that teachers with high levels of knowledge perceived that ADHD negatively impacted upon students' academic and social relationships. Such teachers were more likely to seek help from support services for students with ADHD, with the aim of achieving better outcomes in their classrooms, when compared with teachers whose levels of knowledge about ADHD were low and who thus made naïve judgements about students with the disorder (Legato, 2011).

Hence, if teachers have poor knowledge of this condition, they will not be able to plan effective behavioral strategies (Barkley, 2005). If they have a good understanding of ADHD, it will enable them to change their classroom management, adapt the curriculum, and use a variety of teaching strategies in order to create a positive learning environment (Kleynhans, 2005).

2.3.1 Factors Affecting Teachers' Knowledge

Brook, Watemberg, and Geva (2002) emphasize the importance of training in relation to teachers' knowledge. Their study showed that teachers who did not receive training in dealing with ADHD considered the condition to be the result of parental attitudes. Teachers who had training, on the other hand, showed an understanding of the disorder and its effects on students' behavior (Brook et al., 2002). Another study conducted in Iran, mainly in Isfahan, aimed to show the effectiveness of participation in workshops in terms of school teachers' knowledge and function with regard to students with ADHD (Sarraf, Karahmadi, Marasy, & Azhar, 2011). Additionally, Vereb and DiPerna (2004) stress the positive correlation between teaching experience, teacher training, and teachers' knowledge and understanding of ADHD. Teachers' participation in ADHD training was very helpful in showing them how to apply behavior management strategies (Vereb & DiPerna, 2004). Teaching experience and training have been positively correlated with a greater understanding of children with ADHD (Legato, 2011).

2.4 Gender of Students with ADHD and Teachers' Perceptions

Estimates of the prevalence of ADHD have consistently indicated that boys are diagnosed more frequently that girls (Sciutto, Nolfi, & Bluhm, 2004). Moreover, boys are being referred disproportionally more frequently than girls (Sciutto et al., 2004). Because the behavior of children with ADHD are likely to be observed first of all in the classroom, teachers are essential to the early identification of children in need of referral and support services (Coles, Slavec, Bernstein, & Baroni, 2012). According to Coles et al. (2012), this difference in referral rates may be the result of gender differences in the expression of ADHD symptoms. Boys with ADHD typically show high rates of hyperactivity, disruptiveness, and other externalizing symptoms, which are obvious to teachers. However, girls with ADHD tend to show the ADD subtype, exhibiting low levels of hyperactivity and high levels of inattentiveness, internalizing symptoms, and social impairment. This pattern of symptoms is less likely to disrupt the classroom and, thus, may be overlooked by teachers (Sciutto et al., 2004). Sciutto et al. (2004) investigated the effect of the gender of children with ADHD on teachers' referral decisions. One hundred and ninety-nine teachers from Ohio read profiles of fictional children differing in gender and the types of symptoms they exhibited and rated the likelihood of whether they would refer the children. Results showed that teachers were more likely to refer boys than girls, regardless of the symptom type, but the largest gender difference in referrals was in relation to boys who exhibited hyperactivity (Sciutto et al., 2004). Jackson and King (2004) studied the effect of gender differences on teachers' understanding of ADHD symptoms on 91 teachers in an upper Midwest City. Results of the study showed that teachers' ratings of hyperactivity were significantly concentrated on boys and girls were under-recognized (Jackson & King, 2004). Similarly, another study conducted in England reported under-recognition of ADHD in girls compared with boys and that teachers had difficulty in identifying and poor knowledge about ADHD subtypes (Groenewald, Emond, & Sayal, 2009). However, Maniadaki et al. (2003) emphasize the role that sociocultural expectations may play in creating bias when teachers decide to refer students with ADHD. Bias in teacher referrals are subject to cultural expectations, since in most societies quietness is considered normal for girls, while hyperactivity is regarded as more characteristic of boys.

Therefore, improving teachers' knowledge about ADHD, especially with regard to inattention, could assist in tackling gender issues and avoiding cultural biases linked to a specific gender.

2.5 Conclusion

Definitions of ADHD have evolved gradually, ranging from brain damage syndrome to minimal brain damage, eventually becoming what we today call attention deficit and hyperactivity disorder as defined by the DSM-IV. ADHD affects about 5–7 % of school-aged students in the USA, causing family problems, impeding students' academic achievement, contributing to disruption in the classrooms, and leading to low self-esteem. Teachers are viewed as the most valuable source of help for these students in their classrooms, but without adequate knowledge or training in how to address the need of children with ADHD, teachers may feel unprepared to face the many challenges that such children may present and will be less likely to seek support for their students (Legato, 2011). By identifying the main aspects of ADHD within three specific areas—causes of ADHD, symptoms, and diagnosis of ADHD—and treatment of, and intervention in, ADHD and by highlighting the importance of teachers' knowledge and effective role within these areas, teachers will be able to make more prompt and appropriate referrals and adopt good pre-intervention techniques in order to create a positive learning environment.

The overview of the literature emphasizes the fact that many teachers around the world lack knowledge of and have had very little or no training in ADHD and the possible intervention techniques that can be used in the classroom. The knowledge that most teachers seemed to have gained has been obtained through the media, with many teachers stating that ADHD is a result of parental spoiling. Unfortunately, inaccurate information often leads to inappropriate referrals.

The gender of the child with ADHD has been found to be a factor worthy of exploration when looking at teachers' perceptions of ADHD. What impact does gender have on teachers? Research indicates that there are about 2.5 boys for every girl with ADHD and about six boys for every girl with ADHD referred to clinics in the USA (Ohan & Visser, 2009). According to the literature, teachers in most countries are the ones responsible for making referrals, and these referrals are inappropriate not only because of teachers' lack of knowledge but also due to some cultural bias and misconceptions. ADD girls are under-recognized and, thus, are not referred or diagnosed since quietness is considered to be a normal characteristic in girls. However, boys always have higher rates of hyperactivity and disruptiveness, which makes it easier for the teacher to identify the fact that they may suffer from ADHD and to refer them. The studies interpreting the effects of the gender of students with ADHD on teachers' perceptions support the above and have identified two possible reasons for this gender issue: (1) bias in teacher referrals is subject to cultural expectations since in most societies quietness is considered normal for girls, while boys are more likely to show signs of hyperactivity (Maniadaki et al., 2003) and/or (2) teachers' lack of knowledge of ADHD types. Teachers' failure to understand that ADD is a type of ADHD may explain their inability or difficulty in recognizing girls with ADHD.

Finally, it is important to consider cultural factors when looking at the gender of the student with ADHD, the causes of the condition, and the possible intervention and treatments. When considering the prevalence of ADHD, this depends to a greater extent on the diagnostic criteria that each country uses (Krowski, 2009). Moreover, ADHD causes are still a matter of debate between researchers and practitioners in the medical, genetic, and psychosocial spheres, specifically in the French and US contexts. In addition, teachers' referrals are influenced by their preferences and their cultural expectations of boys and girls. There is a great need for research on ADHD in the Arab world (Farah et al., 2009), particularly in southern Lebanon, which is an unexplored area.

References

Alloway, T., Elliott, J., & Holmes, J. (2010). The prevalence of ADHD-like symptoms in a community sample. *Journal of Attention Disorders, 14*, 52–56.

American Academy of Pediatrics. (2011). ADHD: Clinical practice guideline for the diagnosis, evaluation, and treatment of attention-deficit/hyperactivity disorder in children and adolescents. *Pediatrics, 18*, 1–18.

American Psychiatry Association. (2013). Attention deficit/hyperactivity disorder. Retrieved from: http://www.dsm5.org/Pages/Default.aspx

Amiri, S., Fakhari, A., Maheri, M., & Asl, A. (2010). Attention deficit/hyperactivity disorder in primary school children of Tabriz, north-west Iran. *Paediatric and Perinatal Epidemiology, 24*, 597–601.

Badeleh, M. T. (2013). Attention deficit hyperactivity disorder and elementary teachers' awareness. *Journal of Medical Sciences, 13*, 829–833.

Barkley, R. (2005). *Attention-deficit hyperactivity disorder* (3rd ed.). New York: The Guilford Press.

Barkley, R., & Mash, E. (Eds.). (2006). *Treatment of childhood disorders* (3rd ed.). New York: Guilford Press.

Bell, A. S. (2013). A critical review of ADHD diagnostic criteria: What to address in the DSM-V. *Journal of Attention Disorders, 15*, 3–10.

Brook, U., Watemberg, N., & Geva, D. (2002). Attitude and knowledge of attention deficit hyperactivity disorder and learning disability among high school teachers. *Patient Education and Counseling, 40*, 247–252.

Coles, E. K., Slavec, J., Bernstein, M., & Baroni, E. (2012). Exploring the gender gap in referrals for children with ADHD and other disruptive behavior disorders. *Journal of Attention Disorders, 16*, 101–108.

Farah, L. G., Fayyad, J. A., Eapen, V., Cassir, Y., Salamoun, M. M., Tabet, C. C., et al. (2009). ADHD in the Arab world a review of epidemiologic studies. *Journal of Attention Disorders, 13*, 211–222.

Ghanizadeh, A., Bahredar, M. J., & Moeini, S. R. (2005). Knowledge and attitudes towards attention deficit hyperactivity disorder among elementary school teachers. *Patient Education and Counseling, 63*, 84–88.

Graham, J., Seth, S., & Coghill, D. (2007). *ADHD Medicine, 35*, 181–185.
Gregg, S. (2005). Understanding and identifying children with ADHD. Retrieved from http://www.ldonline.org/article/5974?theme=print
Groenewald, C., Emond, A., & Sayal, K. (2009). Recognition and referral of girls with attention deficit hyperactivity disorder: Case vignette study. *Child: Care, Health and Development, 35*, 767–772.
Guerra, F. R., & Brown, M. S. (2012). Teacher knowledge of attention deficit hyperactivity disorder among middle school students in south Texas. *RMLE Online, 36*, 1–7.
Hong, Y. (2008). Teachers' perceptions of young children with ADHD in Korea. *Early Child Development and Care, 178*, 399–414.
Howe, D. (2010). ADHD and its comorbidity: An example of gene-environment interaction and its implications for child and family social work. *Child and Family Social Work, 15*, 265–275.
Jackson, D. A., & King, A. R. (2004). Gender differences in the effects of oppositional behavior on teacher ratings of ADHD symptoms. *Journal of Abnormal Child Psychology, 32*, 215–224.
Kleynhans, S. E. (2005). Primary school teachers' knowledge and misperceptions of attention deficit hyperactivity disorder. (Unpublished Master's Thesis). University of Stellenbosch, Matieland, South Africa.
Kovshoff, H., Williams, S., Vrijens, M., Danckaerts, M., Thompson, M., Yardley, L., et al. (2012). The decisions regarding ADHD management (DRAMA) study: Uncertainties and complexities in assessment, diagnosis and treatment, from the clinician's point of view. *European Child & Adolescent Psychiatry, 21*, 87–99.
Krowski, K. F. (2009). *ADHD: Urban teachers' knowledge, beliefs and classroom practice*. University of Massachusetts: These and Dissertations. Retrieved from: http://search.proquest.com/docview/305140059?accountid=8555.
Legato, J. (2011). *Effects of teacher factors on expectations of students with ADHD*. DePaul University. Theses and Dissertations. Retrieved from: http://via.library.depaul.edu/etd/66
Maniadaki, K., Sonuga-Barke, E. J. S., & Kakouros, E. (2003). Trainee nursery teachers' perceptions of disruptive behaviour disorders; The effect of sex of child on judgments of typicality and severity. *Child: Care, Health and Development, 29*, 433–440.
Millichap, J. G. (2010). *Attention deficit hyperactivity disorder handbook: A physician's guide to ADHD*. New York: Springer. Retrieved from: http://link.springer.com/book/10.1007%2F978-1-4419-1397-5.
Moon, S. K. (2011). Cultural perspectives on attention deficit hyperactivity disorder: A comparison between Korea and the U.S. *Journal of International Business & Cultural Studies, 6*, 1–11.
Morisoli, K., & McLaughlin, T. F. (2006). Medication and school intervention for elementary students with attention deficit hyperactivity disorder. *International Journal of Special Education, 19*, 97–106.
Nur, N., & Kavakci, O. (2010). Elementary school teachers' knowledge and attitudes related to attention deficit hyperactivity disorder. *Journal of Society for Development in New Net Environment in B&H, 4*, 350–355.
Oh, W., Park, E. S., Suk, M. H., Song, D. H., & Im, Y. (2012). Parenting of children with ADHD in South Korea: The role of socio-emotional development of children with ADHD. *Journal of Clinical Nursing, 21*, 1932–1942.
Ohan, J. L., & Visser, T. A. W. (2009). Why is there a gender gap in children presenting for attention deficit/hyperactivity disorder services? *Journal of Clinical Child and Adolescent Psychology, 38*, 650–660.
Pires, T., da Silva, C. M. F. P., & de Assis, S. G. (2013). Association between family environment and attention deficit hyperactivity disorder in children–mothers' and teachers' views. *BMC Psychiatry, 13*, 624–633.
Salway, M. (2010). Repertoires of ADHD in UK newspaper media. *Health, 15*(5), 533–549.
Sarraf, N., Karahmadi, M., Marasy, M. R., & Azhar, S. M. (2011). A comparative study of the effectiveness of nonattendance and workshop education of primary school teachers in their knowledge, attitude and function towards ADHD students in Isfahan in 2010. *Journal of Research in Medical Sciences, 16*, 1196–1201.

Sciutto, M. J., Nolfi, C. J., & Bluhm, C. (2004). Effects of child gender and symptom type on referrals for ADHD by elementary school teachers. *Journal of Emotional and Behavioral Disorders, 12*, 247–253.

Taylor, E. (2011). Antecedents of ADHD: A historical account of diagnostic concepts. *Attention Deficit and Hyperactivity Disorders, 3*, 69–75.

Vereb, H. L., & DiPerna, J. C. (2004). Teachers' knowledge of ADHD, treatments for ADHD, and treatment acceptability: An initial investigation. *School Psychology Review, 33*, 421–428.

Wedge, M. (2012). Why French kids don't have ADHD. *Psychology Today*. Retrieved from: http://www.psychologytoday.com/blog/suffer-the-children/201203/why-french-kids-dont-have-adhd

Weyandt, L. L., Fulton, K. M., Schepman, S. B., Verdi, G. R., & Wilson, K. G. (2009). Assessment of teacher and school psychologist knowledge of attention deficit/hyperactivity disorder. *Psychology in the Schools, 46*, 951–961.

Chapter 3
Researching Lebanese Teachers' Knowledge and Perceptions of ADHD

3.1 Discovering What Teachers Know and Perceive of ADHD

Our aim in conducting this study was to explore the level of knowledge about ADHD possessed by Lebanese teachers involved in elementary education. We were also keen to find out how the gender of students with ADHD affected such teachers' perceptions of the disorder. Accordingly our specific research questions were as follows: (a) What knowledge do Lebanese teachers in the elementary cycle have about ADHD? (b) How does the gender of students with ADHD affect elementary teachers' perceptions of ADHD?

3.2 Research Design Used to Study Teachers' Knowledge and Perceptions of ADHD

Our study adopted a mixed-methods approach that explored the aims of the research through a combination of quantitative and qualitative measures. Creswell (1998) argues that a mixed-methods research study involves more than a collection and analysis of both quantitative and qualitative data; both approaches are used in conjunction with one another to increase the overall strength of the study. According to Johnson and Onwuegbuzie (2004), the main goal of mixed-methods research is not to replace either of these approaches, but rather to draw on the strengths and minimize the weaknesses of both. While quantitative research can avoid the pitfalls of subjectivity and provide results that can be generalized to a specific population, a qualitative study can ensure an in-depth investigation of a topic (Edmunds, 1999). Therefore, a mixed-methods approach is beneficial in terms of neutralizing or canceling the biases that may arise from using either qualitative or quantitative research alone (Creswell, 1998).

Survey packets were used as a primary data collection tool, and then focus group discussions (FGDs) took place as a secondary form of data collection to follow up and

H.M. Berri, A. Al-Hroub, *ADHD in Lebanese Schools*,
Springer Briefs in Psychology, DOI 10.1007/978-3-319-28700-3_3

confirm the quantitative results. Creswell (1998) defines surveys as means of describing in quantitative terms, trends, attitudes, or opinions of individuals who are representative of a particular population through the administration of questionnaires or conducting structured interviews. In this case, survey research was chosen as it is considered to be the best way to collect data in order to measure teachers' knowledge about ADHD from a population that is too large to observe directly or to make assumptions about (Kleynhans, 2005). According to Kleynhans (2005), there are standard ways of measuring responses to questionnaires or test items which make them amenable to a wide range of statistical manipulations; clearly this is an advantage of such an approach.

In our study, focus group discussions took place after completing the survey packets. A focus group discussion (FGD) can be regarded as a method of qualitative research that tends to be more exploratory than quantitative research (Edmunds, 1999). Merriam (2010), for example, points out that FGDs are best employed to answer the *whys* and *hows* of human behavior. Edmunds (1999) also argues that FGDs can be coordinated, conducted, and analyzed within a relatively short space of time. Additionally, probing and clarification of participants' comments are easy to do in the focus group environment. In this study, FGDs provided an in-depth understanding of teachers' knowledge in relation to ADHD and their perceptions of gender with regard to boys and girls with ADHD, allowing for the capture and evaluation of subjective comments.

3.3 Fifteen Schools in Southern Lebanon

This study focused on 15 schools (six private and nine public) in two areas in southern Lebanon, specifically Saida and Nabatieh. Survey packets were distributed to all these schools, but focus group discussions took place in just two of the schools. All schools in this study provide classes from nursery level through to grade 12 and all implement the Lebanese baccalaureate. There were few differences between public and private schools in both regions. Principally, private schools in this study enriched students' knowledge of languages by teaching French as a second foreign language starting in grade 1. Furthermore, only two of the private schools were well equipped with libraries, computer centers, and auditoria. None of these schools provided special services for students with special educational needs.

3.4 Methods Used to Study Teachers' Knowledge and Perceptions of ADHD in Schools in Lebanon

3.4.1 Teachers of Students with ADHD in Public and Private Schools in Lebanon

A total of 350 surveySurveys were distributed to elementary private and public school teachers in the 15 schools that took part in our study. We received 301 completed surveys in total. The participants who filled the surveys and took part in the

Table 3.1 Composition of sample by gender

Method	Gender	Total
Surveys	Male	0
	Female	301
	Total	301
FGDs	Male	0
	Female	16
	Total	16

Table 3.2 Number of private and public schools

Type of school	Private	Public	Total
Number of schools	6	9	15

focus group discussions consisted of elementary private and public school teachers who had agreed to be involved in the study. They were selected according to the following criteria: they had to be working at the elementary level in a private or public school and teaching any grade from 1 to 6. The researcher used purposive sampling to choose female elementary teachers with different subject specialisms. In fact, only two focus group discussions took place, one in the area of Saida and one in the Nabatieh region. Participation in this study was completely voluntary, and there were eight teachers who participated in each of the FGDs. Table 3.1 below illustrates the number of female teachers who completed the survey and subsequently participated in the FGDs.

Table 3.2 indicates the number of schools selected for this study. The total number of selected schools was 15 schools. Surveys were distributed among six private schools and nine public schools.

3.5 Collecting Data on Teachers' Knowledge and Perceptions of ADHD

Data collection procedures took place in two phases: the first phase involving the administration of individual surveys (demographics, vignettes, KADDS) and the second taking the form of FGDs.

3.5.1 Individual Surveys

After obtaining the Institutional Review Board's (IRB) approval, a letter was sent to the Ministry of Education and Higher Education (MEHE) to explain the nature of the study and acquire permission to conduct it in the selected schools. Another letter was then sent by the researcher to all the school principals asking for their approval for the research to be conducted in their schools with teachers at the elementary level. The recruitment process consisted of two stages: (1) sending out teacher recruitment forms and (2) contacting those teachers who agreed to take part in the study.

The individual surveySurvey packets contained one copy of each measure (demographics, ADHD questionnaire, and four vignettes) in a stapled set under Appendix A. Participants first completed the demographics questionnaire, then the KADDS measures of knowledge, and then rated the vignettes, in that order. After completing the surveys, meetings were arranged for both FGDs to take place.

3.5.2 Demographics and KADDS

The first part of the survey consisted of general information about teachers, including their gender, years of experience, grades that they were teaching, their level of education, and so on. In the second part, teachers had to take the KADDS. This scale was developed by Sciutto, Terjesen, and Frank (2000) and had previously been administered in six New York area schools and also in Australia (Kleynhans, 2005). According to Sciutto et al. (2000), the KADDS has a high internal consistency (0.8–0.9), and in their study a group and an expert group consisting of 40 upper-level doctoral students in clinical and school psychology were used to work on it. The KADDS is a modified 30-item rating scale designed to measure teachers' knowledge about ADHD, as it relates to symptoms and diagnosis of ADHD and general knowledge about the nature, causes, and treatment of ADHD using a series of "true-false-do not know" items (Sciutto et al., 2000).

The teachers participating in our study read statements about ADHD and rated each statement as "true" (T), "false" (F), or "do not know" (DK). According to Legato (2011), the option of choosing helps the researcher to distinguish between teachers' lack of knowledge about ADHD and their misconceptions. KADDS statements refer to both positive and negative indicators of ADHD in order to account for a negative response bias (Legato, 2011). Sample items include "Children with ADHD often fidget or squirm in their seats" (symptoms); "ADHD is more common in the first-degree biological relative (i.e., mother, father) of children with ADHD than in the general population" (causes); "In order to be diagnosed as ADHD, a child must exhibit relevant symptoms in two or more settings (e.g., home, school)" (diagnosis); and "Reducing dietary intake of sugar or food additives is generally effective in reducing the symptoms of ADHD" (treatment) (see Appendix A).

The questionnaire was translated into Arabic by an interpreter. English and Arabic versions of the questionnaire were passed on to the teachers, who were given the option to complete it according to their language preference.

3.5.3 *Vignettes*

According to DSM-IV, there are three subtypes of ADHD: (1) ADHD (combined type), both inattention and hyperactivity-impulsiveness symptoms; (2) ADHD (predominantly inattentive type), inattention, but not enough (at least six out of nine) hyperactivity-impulsiveness symptoms; and (3) ADHD (predominantly hyperactive-impulsive). Teachers' expectations regarding students' gender in relation to ADHD subtypes 2 and 3 were assessed using teachers' responses to questions based on four vignettes. The vignettes described four elementary school-aged students (two males, two females) who exhibited symptoms that clearly met the *Diagnostic and Statistical Manual of Mental Disorders*, 4th edition (DSM-IV) symptom criteria for ADHD that were discussed earlier in the literature section. The two vignettes both addressed DSM-IV subtypes, in particular types 2 and 3. Our aim was to explore how ADHD students' gender would affect teachers' perceptions of these students' subtypes, since there is a significant difference in the way that teachers behave toward boys and girls with ADHD (Ohan & Visser, 2009). In addition, teachers have difficulty in identifying ADHD subtypes. They tend to neglect and under-recognize type 2 (ADD) in girls since girls in general are quiet and docile (Groenewald, Emond, & Sayal, 2009). Teachers even tend to contribute hyperactivity in boys with other disorders (Sciutto et al., 2004). Therefore, the first two vignettes addressed the cases of Jamil and Jamila, a boy and a girl whose behavior was of the hyperactive subtype, while the third and fourth vignettes, likewise, dealt with the cases of Jamil and Jamila, but this time exhibiting inattentive behavior.

For the purpose of this study, Legato's (2011) vignette questions were adapted and modified accordingly by two professors of educational psychology at the American University of Beirut (AUB). These vignettes enabled us to study not only teachers' knowledge about the different subtypes of ADHD but also the underlying bias in teachers' perceptions of boys and girls in a Lebanese context.

An identical set of nine questions accompanied each vignette with only the name of the child who was the subject of the vignette being changed. Teachers provided a rating in response to each question on a Likert-type scale from 1 to 3, with 1 representing "not at all," 2 representing "moderately," and 3 meaning "extremely." The first four questions assessed teachers' perceptions of each child in relation to hyperactivity symptoms, the impact of such symptoms on students' daily life and school work, and the effect of the Lebanese culture on their views. Questions 5, 6, and 7 focused on teachers' readiness to deal with the students' behavior while question 8 examined teachers' confidence when it came to implementing an intervention plan for each child. Question 9 considered teachers' ability to identify a student with ADHD in two respects: first, their ability to differentiate between ADHD and other discords and, second, their competence in recognizing ADHD subtypes in relation to gender and the Lebanese culture (see Appendix A).

3.6 Focus Groups: Teachers Discuss Their Knowledge and Perceptions of ADHD

FGDs are rapid assessments that enable the researcher to obtain insights into target audience's perceptions, needs, problems, beliefs, and reasons for certain practices (Escalada, 2009). In our study, FGDs enabled the researcher to collect data on teachers' perceptions and knowledge of ADHD and its symptoms and their role as teachers in the process of identifying boys and girls with the condition and providing them with assistance. The discussions involving eight teachers in each case took place in the libraries of two different schools at agreed times, and each FGD lasted for 1 h (Rennekamp & Nall, 2003). The session started with the moderator welcoming the group, introducing herself and the assistant moderator, who was responsible for tape-recording the discussion (Rennekamp & Nall, 2003). The moderator explained the purpose of the FGD and the ground rules for participation, the main ones being as follows: there are no right or wrong answers to questions; viewpoints are to be respected; no names will be included in any report and all comments and responses are to remain confidential; everyone is expected to participate and to give others the opportunity to do so; and having side conversations are to be avoided. After that, the discussion moved from general to specific issues on two main themes: the concept/definition of ADHD, including its causes and the symptoms and characteristics to be considered when making a diagnosis, and procedures used in identifying boys and girls with the disorder and the identification procedures for boys and girls accompanied by the possible assistance these teachers might provide for students with ADHD (see Appendix B).

3.7 Analyzing Data Collected from Teachers

The statistical software that was employed to analyze the data collected from the demographic questionnaire was the Statistical Package for Social Sciences (SPSS). It was used to generate descriptive statistics relating to the personal of the participant teachers.

To measure teachers' knowledge of ADHD, their ratings of the KADDS statements as "true," "false," or "do not know" produced stores for each of the subscales. These were used to calculate percentages and averages using the Excel program, which was also used to produce percentages based on teachers' ratings of each of the vignettes.

As for the FGDs, we developed a general coding protocol by categorizing the emerging data. The data were analyzed as they had been collected. Thus, data analysis was conducted simultaneously as data collection (Corbin & Strauss, 2008). We identified constructs, themes, and patterns that best explained the data collected within and across groups of participants. We compared the codes that emerged across segments, with the aim of discovering commonalities that reflected the underlying meaning of, and the relationships between, the coded data, in order to answer the research questions and fulfill the purpose of the study (Corbin & Strauss, 2008). In this way, the data interpretation helped us to discover the common conceptions and misconceptions that teachers have about ADHD students.

3.8 Evaluation of Results of Research on Teachers' Knowledge and Perceptions of ADHD

We used three criteria to evaluate our study: usefulness, the chain of evidence, and contextual completeness. Because there are no common criteria which were used to identify students with ADHD in Lebanon, the findings of this study may be considered useful. No other studies with this end in view have been conducted. The results of the study may help policy-makers devise a plan to help students with ADHD. In order to test the chain of events, we kept a written record that documented all of the data collection and analysis procedures and clearly defined and related them to each other. Other researchers can, therefore, use the same methodology to replicate the study. Finally, in order to check for contextual completeness, we provided an in-depth description of the history, setting, and research participants.

References

Corbin, J., & Strauss, A. L. (2008). *Basics of qualitative research: Techniques and procedures for developing grounded theory* (3rd ed.). Los Angeles, CA: Sage Publications.

Creswell, J. W. (1998). *Qualitative inquiry and research design: Choosing among five traditions*. Newbury Park, CA: Sage Publications.

Edmunds, H. (1999). *The focus group research handbook*. Lincolnwood, IL: NTC Business Books.

Escalada, M. (2009). DC132: *Focus group discussion*. [handout 7]. Retrieved from http://www.academia.edu/4574254/Focus_Group_Discussion_1

Groenewald, C., Emond, A., & Sayal, K. (2009). Recognition and referral of girls with attention deficit hyperactivity disorder: Case vignette study. *Child: Care, Health and Development, 35*, 767–772.

Johnson, R., & Onwuegbuzie, A. (2004). Mixed methods research: A research paradigm whose time has come. *Educational Researcher, 33*, 14–26.

Kleynhans, S. E. (2005). *Primary school teachers' knowledge and misperceptions of attention deficit hyperactivity disorder*. Unpublished Master's Thesis. University of Stellenbosch, Matieland, South Africa.

Legato, J. (2011). *Effects of teacher factors on expectations of students with ADHD*. DePaul University. Theses and Dissertations. Retrieved from: http://via.library.depaul.edu/etd/66

Merriam, S. B. (2010). *Qualitative research and case study applications in education: Revised and expanded from case study research in education*. San Francisco, CA: Jossey Bass Publishers.

Ohan, J. L., & Visser, T. A. W. (2009). Why is there a gender gap in children presenting for attention deficit/hyperactivity disorder services? *Journal of Clinical Child and Adolescent Psychology, 38*, 650–660.

Rennekamp, R., & Nall, M. (2003). *Using focus groups in program development and evaluation* [handout]. Retrieved from: http://www2.ca.uky.edu/AgPSD/Focus.pdf

Sciutto, M. J., Nolfi, C. J., & Bluhm, C. (2004). Effects of child gender and symptom type on referrals for ADHD by elementary school teachers. *Journal of Emotional and Behavioral Disorders, 12*, 247–253.

Sciutto, M. J., Terjesen, M. D., & Frank, A. S. B. (2000). Teachers' knowledge and misperceptions of attention-deficit/hyperactivity disorder. *Psychology in the Schools, 37*, 115–122.

Chapter 4
Teachers' Knowledge of ADHD and Perceptions of the Behavior of Individual Students with ADHD in Relation to Gender and Culture

4.1 Teachers' Performance in KADDS

The total scores and percentages of the "correct," "incorrect," and "do not know" responses of the 301 teachers to each of the 30 KADDS questions are presented in three tables, each one focusing on the three domains described above.

4.1.1 General Knowledge About ADHD

Responses to statement 9 revealed that more than half of the teachers (54 %) were knowledgeable of the possibility for an adult being diagnosed with ADHD and 43 % of the respondents knew that the prevalence of ADHD in males and females is not equivalent (statement 22). A high percentage of teachers (74 %) were also fairly aware of the fact that a child with ADHD would be more easily identifiable in a classroom setting than in a free play situation (statement 24). In addition, responses to statement 25 showed that teachers (51 %) were aware that the majority of ADHD children performed poorly at school in the elementary years. Table 4.1 shows Lebanese teachers' responses with respect to the general knowledge subscale.

The data show that participants lacked knowledge and held misconceptions about the fact that a child with ADHD may play video games for a long time but will be unable to complete his\her homework. Forty-two percent of teachers held misconceptions about this, while 14 % showed lack of knowledge with regard to this (statement 16). Statement 4 refers to the causes of ADHD and the fact that genetics is a great contributor to ADHD. Twenty-nine percent of respondents had misconceptions relating to this, while 35 % revealed a lack of knowledge. Situational variation in the behavior of children with ADHD in familiar versus unfamiliar situations is the subject of statement 20. Fifty-six percent of the teachers incorrectly

H.M. Berri, A. Al-Hroub, *ADHD in Lebanese Schools*,
Springer Briefs in Psychology, DOI 10.1007/978-3-319-28700-3_4

Table 4.1 Teachers' performance on general knowledge subscale

Questions	Correct response	Correct		Incorrect		Don't know (DK)		Total
		n	%	*n*	%	*n*	%	*N*
4. ADHD is more common in first degree biological relatives (i.e., mother, father) of children with ADHD than in the general population	T	106	35	87	29	104	35	297
9. It is possible for an adult to be diagnosed with ADHD	T	164	54	37	12	95	32	296
12. Symptoms of depression are found more frequently in children with ADHD than in non-ADHD children	T	112	37	83	28	105	35	300
14. Most children with ADHD "outgrow" their symptoms by the onset of puberty and subsequently function normally in adulthood	F	91	30	74	25	135	45	300
16. If a child with ADHD is able to demonstrate sustained attention to video games or TV for over an hour, that child is also able to sustain attention for at least an hour of class or homework	F	129	43	126	42	43	14	298
18. A diagnosis of ADHD by itself makes a child eligible for placement in special education	F	115	38	91	30	93	31	299
20. Children with ADHD generally experience more problems in novel situations than in familiar situations	F	60	20	168	56	67	22	295
21. There are specific physical features which can be identified by medical doctors (e.g., pediatricians) in making a definitive diagnosis of ADHD	F	81	27	133	44	82	27	296
22. In school-age children, the prevalence of ADHD in males and females is equivalent	F	129	43	67	22	104	35	300
23. In very young children (less than 4 years old), the problem behaviors of children with ADHD (e.g., hyperactivity, inattention) are distinctly different from age-appropriate behaviors of non-ADHD children	F	39	13	163	54	97	32	299
24. Children with ADHD are more distinguishable from normal children in a classroom setting than in a free play situation	T	223	74	43	14	32	11	298

(continued)

Table 4.1 (continued)

Questions	Correct response	Correct		Incorrect		Don't know (DK)		Total
		n	%	*n*	%	*n*	%	*N*
25. The majority of ADHD children evidence some degree of poor school performance in the elementary school years	T	155	51	76	25	63	21	294
26. Symptoms of ADHD are often seen in non-ADHD children who come from inadequate and chaotic home environments	T	106	35	124	41	68	23	298
30. Children with ADHD generally display an inflexible adherence to specific routines or rituals	F	29	10	197	66	70	23	296
Average		110	36	105	35	83	28	

Note: Some totals are below 301 as some teachers did not respond to the item

believed that ADHD children are likely to experience more problems in unfamiliar situations than in familiar ones, while 22 % proved to be lacking in knowledge. Additionally, statement 14, which focused on the long-term outcome of ADHD, showed confusions in respondents' answers. Twenty-five percent of the teachers falsely thought that children with ADHD would "outgrow" their symptoms by puberty and would subsequently function normally in adulthood, while 45 % of teachers indicated that they did not know whether this would be the case. A high percentage of teachers (65 %) in this study incorrectly believed that children with ADHD display an inflexible adherence to specific routines or rituals and 23 % responded by choosing the "do not know" option (statement 30). There seemed to be incorrect views and lack of knowledge about the influence of home situations on children with ADHD, with 41 % of teachers holding the belief that symptoms of ADHD are often seen in children without ADHD whose home environments are chaotic and inadequate and 23 % indicating a lack of knowledge (statement 26). In addition to the above, more than half of the participants (54 %) wrongly considered that in very young children, the problem behavior of children with ADHD is distinctly different from the age-appropriate behavior of children without ADHD, and 32 % responded indicating that they did not know (statement 23). In the case of statement 21, teachers (44 %) were also under the false impression that medical doctors are able to make a definitive diagnosis of ADHD, with 27 % were lacking in knowledge. Thirty-nine percent of teachers were also confused regarding the fact that depression is found more frequently in children with ADHD than in those without the condition (statement 12), and 28 % knew little about this. Some participants (30 %) also wrongly believed the premise of statement 18 that the diagnosis of ADHD makes a child eligible for placement in special education, while 31 % of teachers selected the "do not know" response.

4.1.2 Diagnosis and Symptoms

Teachers were very knowledgeable about the symptoms of ADHD, with 76 % of participants aware that ADHD children are frequently distracted by extraneous stimuli (statement 2), 83 % of respondents correctly identified these children as being fidgety and squirming in their seats (statement 7), and 79 % of teachers showing that they were knowledgeable about the two clusters of symptoms (statement 11). Furthermore, a high percentage of teachers (83 %) were aware that the symptoms of ADHD have to be present in two or more settings before a firm diagnosis can be made (statement 15) and nearly 80 % of teachers knew that ADHD children have problems when it comes to organizing tasks and activities (statement 19). Additionally, responses to statement 3 showed that teachers (63 %) were aware of the fact that a child's symptoms must be present before the age of 7 in order to be diagnosed with ADHD. Table 4.2 shows teachers' performance on the diagnosis and symptoms subscale.

Forty-eight percent of teachers had some misunderstandings, and 28 % lacked knowledge in relation to statement 8 which concerned the fact that children with ADHD have an inflated sense of self-esteem and their own importance. In addition, teachers in this study seemed to confuse symptoms of ADHD with symptoms of conduct disorder: 36 % of participants were under the false impression that ADHD children often have a history of stealing or destroying other people's possessions and 28 % indicated that they knew little about this (statement 10). Teachers also proved to have incorrect views about the nature of ADHD children, with 45 % believing that being physically cruel to other people is a symptom of ADHD and 19 % choosing the "do not know" response to statement 5.

4.1.3 Treatment

A majority of responses (68 %) to statement 28 were aware that punishment is not the most effective treatment in reducing the symptoms of ADHD. However, teachers lacked knowledge about the causes of ADHD, and this then influenced their views about treatment. Nearly 50 % of teachers wrongly considered that ADHD is the result of ineffective parenting skills, and 21 % showed a lack of knowledge about the subject of statement 1. Teachers were also unaware of the effect of antidepressant drugs in reducing symptoms of ADHD, with 28 % indicating incorrect beliefs and 47 % proving to have little awareness of the treatment referred to in statement 6. Table 4.3 shows teachers' performance on treatment subscale.

Fifty-eight percent of the respondents to statement 17 were under the misconception that dietary intake of sugar and food additives will effectively reduce the symptoms of ADHD, but 24 % showed no awareness of the role of diet. Moreover, teachers were confused about whether or not individual psychotherapy alone is an adequate treatment for children with ADHD: 31 % of teachers, incorrectly, thought

Table 4.2 Teachers' performance on diagnosis and symptoms subscale

Questions	Correct response	Correct		Incorrect		Don't know (DK)		Total
		n	%	*n*	%	*n*	%	*N*
2. Children with ADHD are frequently distracted by extraneous stimuli	T	229	76	43	14	25	8	297
3. In order to be diagnosed with ADHD, the child's symptoms must have been present before age 7	T	191	63	49	16	60	20	300
5. One symptom of children with ADHD is that they have been physically cruel to other people	F	108	36	134	46	58	19	300
7. Children with ADHD often fidget or squirm in their seats	T	250	83	30	10	20	7	300
8. It is common for children with ADHD to have an inflated sense of self-esteem or their own importance	F	85	28	144	48	60	20	289
10. Children with ADHD often have a history of stealing or destroying other people's things	F	103	34	109	36	84	28	296
11. Current wisdom about ADHD suggests two clusters of symptoms: one of inattention and another consisting of hyperactivity/impulsiveness	T	238	79	3	1	58	19	299
15. In order to be diagnosed as ADHD, a child must exhibit relevant symptoms in two or more settings (e.g., home, school)	T	250	83	8	3	41	14	299
19. Children with ADHD often have difficulty organizing tasks and activities	T	232	77	31	10	21	7	284
Average		187	62	61	20	47	16	

Note: Some totals are below 301 as some teachers did not respond to those items

it was sufficient and 33 % indicated that they had no knowledge (statement 13). Some teachers in this study (41 %) mistakenly held the view that behavioral/psychological interventions for children with ADHD focused primarily on inattention, and 29 % had no knowledge of such interventions (statement 27). As responses to statement 29 showed, almost half of the participants (46 %) thought incorrectly that the use of stimulant medication leads to increased addiction in adulthood, and 41 % indicated that they knew nothing about the effects of such medication. Figure 4.1 is a visual presentation of the results reported in tables. It presents frequencies for teachers' "correct," "incorrect," and "do not know" responses.

As the tables and figure above show, the survey results relate to the three subscales of teachers' general knowledge of ADHD, symptoms/diagnosis of ADHD, and treatments for ADHD. Analysis results reported frequencies of correct answers ranging from 32 % in relation to treatment, 36 % with regard to general knowledge, and 62 % for teachers' knowledge about diagnosis and symptoms of ADHD. Results

Table 4.3 Teachers' performance on treatment subscale

Questions	Correct response	Correct		Incorrect		Don't know (DK)		Total
		n	%	*n*	%	*n*	%	*N*
1. Current research suggests that ADHD is largely the result of ineffective parenting skills	F	139	36	98	47	63	21	300
6. Antidepressant drugs have been effective in reducing symptoms for many children with ADHD	T	70	23	83	28	141	47	294
13. Individual psychotherapy is usually sufficient for the treatment of children with ADHD	F	106	35	92	31	99	33	297
17. Reducing dietary intake of sugar or food additives is generally effective in reducing the symptoms of ADHD	F	55	18	175	58	71	24	301
27. Behavioral/psychological interventions for children with ADHD focus primarily on the child's problems with inattention	F	85	28	124	41	86	29	295
28. Treatments for ADHD which focus primarily on punishment have been found to be the most effective in reducing the symptoms of ADHD	F	204	68	53	18	43	14	300
29. Research has shown that prolonged use of stimulant medication leads to increased addiction (i.e., drug, alcohol) in adulthood	F	39	13	137	46	124	41	300
Average		100	32	109	38	90	30	

Note: Some totals are below 301 as some teachers did not respond to the item

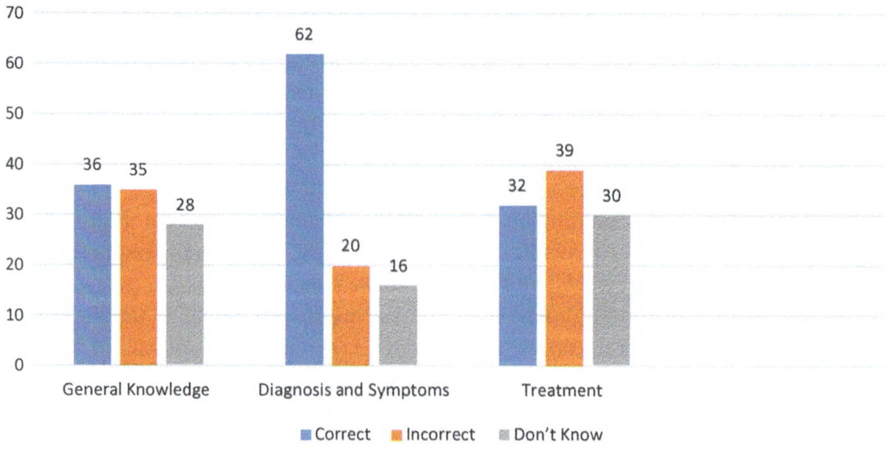

Fig. 4.1 Frequencies for teachers' responses on KADDS

show that teachers seemed to be most knowledgeable about the diagnosis/symptoms of the condition. Frequencies for incorrect answers ranged from 20 % for diagnosis/symptoms, 35 % for general knowledge, and 39 % for treatment. This implies that the level of teachers' misconceptions was highest in the treatment subscale (39 %), with a very similar percentage of incorrect responses in relation to general knowledge (35 %). Frequencies for "do not know" responses varied from 30 % of teachers choosing this response in the treatment subscale to 28 % indicating that they lacked general knowledge about ADHD and 16 % revealing their deficiency of knowledge in diagnosis/symptoms subscale.

4.2 Teachers' Expectations in Relation to Gender

In this section, teachers' responses relating to four vignettes that address two subtypes of ADHD are analyzed. Teachers provided a rating in answer to each question on a Likert-type scale ranging from 1 to 3 as shown below in Table 4.4. Two themes surfaced in the findings: teachers' perceptions of each case that related specifically to Lebanese culture and teachers' readiness to deal with each of these cases. The last question relating to the vignettes (Q9) assessed teachers' ability to identify an ADHD student. These vignettes enabled us to study not only teachers' knowledge about the subtypes of ADHD but also the underlying biases that teachers exhibited toward boys and girls, respectively, in a Lebanese context. Table 4.4 presents teachers' responses with regard to the vignette portraying Jamil, a hyperactive student.

Table 4.4 Teachers' responses to vignette 1

Vignette 1						
	Not at all		Moderately		Extremely	
Item	*n*	%	*n*	%	*n*	%
1. How serious is Jamil's behavior?	54	18	93	31	51	50
2. To what extent would Jamil's behavior affect his ability make friends?	76	25	181	60	41	14
3. To what extent Jamil's behavior hinder his academic progress?	20	7	79	26	199	66
4. How much of Jamil's behavior is common in Lebanese culture?	6	2	211	70	79	26
5. How ready are you to deal with Jamil's behavior in your classroom?	36	12	194	64	68	23
6. How stressful would it be to have Jamil as a student?	16	5	142	47	140	47
7. Do you think that you need to provide Jamil with more attention than you give others?	14	5	94	31	186	62
8. How confident are you about implementing an effective behavior plan for Jamil?	49	16	157	52	94	31

4.2.1 Teachers' Perception of Jamil's Behavior in Vignette 1

Analysis of responses to questions 1, 2, 3, and 4 revealed teachers' perceptions of Jamil's behavior. As shown in Table 4.4, half of the respondents (50 %) perceived his behavior as extremely serious and 31 % of teachers regarded it as moderate. The majority of teachers (60 %) also believed that the boy's behavior would, to a moderate degree, enable him to make friends, while 25 % felt that Jamil would be unable to develop friendships at all with such behavior. Moreover, more than half of the teachers (66 %) agreed that Jamil's behavior would hinder his academic progress. Nearly 70 % of respondents also viewed his behavior as moderately common in Lebanese culture.

4.2.2 Teachers' Readiness to Manage Jamil's Behavior in Vignette 1

Questions 5, 6, 7, and 8 in vignette 1 were analyzed to determine teachers' readiness to manage Jamil's behavior. According to Table 4.4, just under two-thirds of the teachers (64 %) believed that they would be moderately ready to address Jamil's behavior in their classrooms, but 23 % of respondents considered that they could be extremely well prepared. In addition, 47 % of teachers thought that it would be moderately stressful to have to cope with a student like Jamil. However, 47 % felt that having Jamil in their classroom would be extremely stressful and he would need to be given a much greater amount of attention than other students received (62 %). Of 301 teachers, more than half (52 %) felt themselves to be moderately ready to implement an effective behavioral plan for Jamil, but 16 % did not perceive themselves to be prepared at all. Teachers' interpretations of, and beliefs about, Jamil's case varied among respondents (question 9). Table 4.5 presents teachers' personal beliefs in relation to the Jamil scenario.

Teachers' opinions about Jamil's case varied as shown in Table 4.5, with the most common response (20 %) showing awareness that the description of Jamil's behavior in the vignette portrays a case of hyperactivity. A similar proportion, 18 % of teachers, attributed Jamil's behavior to an ADHD disorder without referring to the specific subtype of the condition. Some respondents (12 %) believed that Jamil was suffering from psychological problems. Moreover, 8 % of teachers thought that Jamil was just in need of care. Similarly, 8 % of respondents regarded his behavior to be a result of being spoiled. Opinions varied among other respondents, some deeming Jamil to be a child who had family problems (6 %), some viewing him as an attention seeker (5 %), and others seeing him as undisciplined (4 %). A small percentage (4 %) referred to him as an aggressive child, in need of love, clumsy, and dangerous. Some teachers (12 %) chose the "do not know" response and 4 % did not respond at all. Table 4.6 reports teachers' responses to the vignette describing the behavior of Jamila, a hyperactive student.

Table 4.5 Teachers' beliefs about Jamil's case

Vignette 1		
Responses	Number of responses	%
Hyperactivity	61	20
ADHD	54	18
Has psychological problems	32	12
Needs care	25	8
Spoiled	25	8
Family problems	18	6
Attention seeker	15	5
No discipline	12	4
Others (aggressive, in need of love, clumsy, dangerous)	12	4
Don't know (DK)	35	12
No response	12	4
Total	301	101

Note: The total percentage is more than 100 because of rounding up

Table 4.6 Teachers' responses to vignette 2

Vignette 2						
	Not at all		Moderately		Extremely	
Item	*n*	%	*n*	%	*n*	%
1. How serious is Jamila's behavior?	49	16	91	30	153	51
2. To what extent would Jamila's behavior affect her ability to make friends?	75	25	172	57	44	15
3. To what extent Jamila's behavior hinder her academic progress?	12	4	94	31	188	62
4. How much of Jamila's behavior is common in Lebanese culture?	7	2	237	79	49	16
5. How ready are you to deal with Jamila's behavior in your classroom?	28	9	198	66	69	23
6. How stressful would it be to have Jamila as a student?	21	7	139	46	135	45
7. Do you think that you need to provide Jamila with more attention than you give others?	15	5	98	33	182	60
8. How confident are you about implementing an effective behavior plan for Jamila?	48	16	174	58	72	24

4.2.3 Teachers' Perception of Jamila's Behavior in Vignette 2

As mentioned in the previous vignette, questions 1, 2, 3, and 4 were analyzed to discover teachers' perceptions of the student's behavior. As Table 4.6 shows, half of the respondents (51 %) regarded Jamila's behavior as extremely serious, although 30 % of teachers saw it as only moderately serious. Some teachers (57 %) also believed that Jamila's behavior would moderately affect her ability to make friends, while 25 % considered that Jamila would be unable to make friends at all with such behavior. Furthermore, 62 % of teachers were in agreement that Jamila's behavior would greatly hinder her academic progress. The majority of respondents (79 %) also viewed Jamila's behavior as moderately common in Lebanese culture.

4.2.4 Teachers' Readiness to Manage Jamila's Behavior in Vignette 2

Responses to questions 5, 6, 7, and 8 were analyzed to discover how prepared teachers would be to manage Jamila's behavior. According to Table 4.6, more than half of the teachers (66 %) believed that they would be ready, to a moderate extent, to deal with Jamila's behavior in their classrooms and 23 % of respondents considered that they would be very ready. In addition, 46 % of teachers felt that it would be moderately stressful to have a student like Jamila in the class and 45 % believed that Jamila's presence in the class would be extremely stressful. The majority, 60 %, strongly agreed that she would need to be given more attention than that accorded to other students. More than half of the teachers (58 %) regarded themselves as moderately ready to implement an effective behavior plan for Jamila, but 16 % perceived themselves as completely unprepared. Table 4.7 presents teachers' evaluations of Jamila's case (question 9).

Teachers presented a variety of views in relation to Jamila's case, as shown in Table 4.7, with 27 % of respondents recognizing Jamila as hyperactive. Other teachers (9 %) identified Jamila as a child with ADHD without referring to which specific subtype of ADHD. Eight percent of respondents were of the opinion that Jamila needed care. There was a variety of other responses, with 7 % of teachers believing

Table 4.7 Teachers' beliefs about Jamila's case

Vignette 2		
Responses	Number of responses	%
Hyperactivity	81	27
ADHD	28	9
Needs care	24	8
Has psychological problems	22	7
Careless	15	5
Low achiever	14	5
Spoiled	11	4
Others (messy, aggressive, active, bad)	50	17
Do not know (DK)	29	10
No response	27	9
Total	301	101

Note: The total percentage is more than 100 because of rounding that Jamila had psychological problems, 5 % regarding her as careless, 5 % perceiving her as a low achiever, and 4 % viewing her as spoiled. Others (17 %) described her as messy, aggressive, active, bad, and lazy. Some teachers (10 %) selected the "do not know" option and 9 % offered no response.

4.2.5 Teachers' Perceptions of Hyperactivity in Vignettes 1 and 2

Tables 4.4 and 4.6 showed teachers' ratings for Jamil and Jamila, both of whom exhibited hyperactive behavior. Teachers' ratings for both vignettes differed little in relation to gender. Half of the participants (50 %) regarded Jamil's behavior as extremely serious and almost the same percentage (51 %) held the same belief about Jamila's behavior. A majority of teachers (60 %) perceived that Jamil's behavior would only moderately affect his ability to make friends and 57 % of teachers believed the same with regard to Jamila. More than half of teachers (66 %) rated Jamil's behavior as extremely like to hinder his academic progress, with 68 % of teachers according the same rating to Jamila. Seventy percent of teachers viewed Jamil's behavior as moderately common in Lebanese society, and 78 % also perceived Jamila's hyperactivity as moderately common in the Lebanese context. Sixty-four percent of teachers considered that they were moderately prepared to deal with Jamil's behavior in their classroom, and 66 % produced the same rating for Jamila. Some teachers, 47 % for Jamil and 45 % for Jamila, agreed that it would be extremely stressful to have these students as members of the class. In addition, 62 % of teachers felt that Jamil, to a great extent, would need more attention than other students might require. Similarly, 60 % of teachers believed likewise about Jamila. More than half (52 %) of respondents regarded themselves as moderately ready to implement an effective behavior plan for Jamil, with 58 % believing the same with respect to Jamila. Teachers' ratings of hyperactivity symptoms did not seem to differ in terms of gender, and their perceptions of hyperactivity were apparently unaffected by the fact that Jamil was a boy and Jamila, a girl.

Table 4.8 reports teachers' ratings with regard to Jamil as an ADD student.

4.2.6 Teachers' Perception of Jamil's Behavior in Vignette 3

Teachers' responses to questions 1, 2, 3, and 4 were analyzed in order to reveal their perceptions of Jamil's behavior. Table 4.8 shows that 49 % of the respondents perceived Jamil's behavior as moderately serious, 27 % viewed it as extremely serious, and 22 % did not regard it as serious at all. A majority of teachers (63 %) also believed that Jamil's behavior would moderately affect his capacity to make friends, but 21 % of respondents believed that Jamil would be unable

Table 4.8 Teachers' responses to vignette 3

Vignette 3						
	Not at all		Moderately		Extremely	
Item	*n*	%	*n*	%	*n*	%
1. How serious is Jamil's behavior?	67	22	147	49	82	27
2. To what extent would Jamil's behavior affect his ability to make friends?	64	21	191	63	41	14
3. To what extent Jamil's behavior hinder his academic progress?	19	6	148	49		43
4. How much of Jamil's behavior is common in Lebanese culture?	8	3	224	74	62	21
5. How ready are you to deal with Jamil's behavior in your classroom?	17	6	175	58	102	34
6. How stressful would it be to have Jamil as a student?	109	36	127	42	59	20
7. Do you think that you need to provide Jamil with more attention than you give others?	13	4	107	36	75	58
8. How confident are you about implementing an effective behavior plan for Jamil?	39	13	149	50	07	36

to form any friendships with such behavior. Nearly half of the teachers (49 %) agreed that Jamil's behavior would moderately hinder his academic progress, and 43 % believed that his academic achievement would be greatly hampered as a result of his behavior. A large proportion of respondents (74 %) also viewed his behavior as moderately common in Lebanese culture, with 21 % perceiving it to be extremely.

4.2.7 *Teachers' Readiness to Manage Jamil's Behavior in Vignette 3*

Answers to questions 5, 6, 7, and 8 of vignette 3 were analyzed to determine how ready teachers would be to manage Jamil's behavior. According to Table 4.8, more than half of the teachers (58 %) believed that they would be moderately ready to deal with Jamil's behavior in their classrooms, and 34 % of respondents believed themselves to be very well prepared. In addition, 42 % of teachers felt that it would be moderately stressful to have to cope with a student like Jamil; however, 36 % did not perceive that having Jamil in their classroom would be at all stressful. The opinion of some respondents (58 %) was that there was a strong need for Jamil to be provided with more attention than that given to other students. Half of the teachers (50 %) also considered themselves moderately ready to implement an effective behavior plan for Jamil, 36 % believed that they were extremely well prepared, and 13 % perceived themselves as quite unprepared to implement such as plan effectively.

Table 4.9 Teachers' beliefs about Jamil's case

Vignette 3		
Responses	Number of responses	%
Inattention	50	17
Dreamer	35	12
Autism	32	11
Needs care	30	10
Quiet	22	7
Slow learner	16	5
Normal child	15	5
Hyper	12	4
Needs to play games	10	3
Family problems	10	3
Others (e.g., shy, lazy, needs love)	23	8
Do not know (DK)	24	8
No response	22	7
Total	301	100

Teachers' interpretations and beliefs about Jamil's case varied (question 9). Table 4.9 presents teachers' personal beliefs in relation to Jamil's scenario.

Teachers' opinions about Jamil's case varied, as shown in Table 4.9, with 17 % of teachers recognizing that Jamil was a boy with attention deficit disorder, 12 % of teachers perceiving him to be a dreamer boy, 11 % thought he was autistic, and some (10 %) considered that he was just in need of care. Seven percent of teachers regarded Jamil as a quiet boy and 5 % thought of Jamil as a slow learner. Other teachers gave a variety of responses, seeing Jamil as a normal child (5 %), as hyper (4 %), as needing to play games (3 %), and as having family problems (3 %). Some (8 %) felt that he was shy, lazy, and in need of love. Finally, 8 % of respondents indicated that they did not know what Jamil's behavior represented and 7 % failed to respond at all.

Table 4.10 displays the responses teachers provided in answer to questions about vignette 4, portraying Jamila as an ADD student.

4.2.8 *Teachers' Perception of Jamila's Behavior in Vignette 4*

As mentioned in relation to previous vignettes, questions 1, 2, 3, and 4 were analyzed to discover how teachers perceived Jamila's behavior. As Table 4.10 shows, half (50 %) of the respondents considered Jamila's behavior to be moderately serious, but 26 % did not agree, seeing her behavior as not serious at all. A majority of teachers (64 %) also believed that Jamila's behavior would moderately undermine her ability to make friends, and 21 % believed that she would fail to make any friends at all because of her behavior. Half of the teachers (50 %) felt that her

Table 4.10 Teachers' responses to vignette 4

Vignette 4

	Not at all		Moderately		Extremely	
Item	*n*	%	*n*	%	*n*	%
1. How serious is Jamila's behavior?	79	26	149	50	62	21
2. To what extent would Jamila's behavior affect her ability to make friends?	62	21	192	64	41	14
3. To what extent Jamila's behavior hinder her academic progress?	30	10	150	50	15	38
4. How much of Jamila's behavior is common in Lebanese culture?	10	3	238	79	49	16
5. How ready are you to deal with Jamila's behavior in your classroom?	19	6	177	59	00	33
6. How stressful would it be to have Jamila as a student?	105	35	137	46	50	17
7. Do you think that you need to provide Jamila with more attention than you give others?	5	2	110	37	74	58
8. How confident are you about implementing an effective behavior plan for Jamila?	30	10	157	52	103	34

academic progress would be hindered to a moderate extent as a result of her behavior, and 38 % believed that such behavior would have a very strong negative impact upon her academic achievement. Respondents (79 %) also viewed Jamila's behavior as moderately common in Lebanese society.

4.2.9 *Teachers' Readiness to Manage Jamila's Behavior in Vignettes 4*

Questions 5, 6, 7, and 8 were analyzed to determine teachers' readiness to manage Jamila's behavior. According to Table 4.10, more than half of the teachers (59 %) believed that they were moderately ready to deal with Jamila's behavior in their classrooms, and 33 % of respondents considered themselves very able to do so. In addition, 46 % of the teachers thought that it would be moderately stressful to have to deal with a student like Jamila, but 35 % did not regard having such a student in class as stressful at all. A majority of respondents (58 %) were of the opinion that Jamila would need to be given much more attention than they paid to others. More than half of teachers (52 %) were moderately confident about implementing an effective behavioral plan for Jamila, and 34 % perceived themselves to be extremely ready to do so.

Teachers' interpretations and beliefs about Jamila's case varied (question 9). Table 4.11 presents their personal beliefs in relation to Jamila's scenario.

Teachers provided a variety of opinions about Jamila's case, as shown in Table 4.11, with 15 % of respondents realizing that Jamila's case was one of

Table 4.11 Teachers' beliefs about Jamila's case

Vignette 4		
Responses	Number of responses	%
Inattention	44	15
Autism	35	12
Dreamer	29	10
Low self-confidence	22	7
Quiet	18	6
Normal child	17	6
Needs care	17	6
Hyperactive	15	5
Careless	13	4
Has a problem	8	3
Lonely	8	3
Others (e.g., poverty, worried, needs love)	15	5
Do not know (DK)	31	10
No response	29	10
Total	301	101

Note: The total percentage is higher than 100 because of rounding up

inattention. A proportion of teachers (12 %) suggested that Jamila was autistic, and 10 % perceived her as a dreamer. Some teachers (7 %) thought that Jamila had low self-confidence, while 6 % thought she was just a quiet child and 6 % perceived her as normal. A further 6 % saw her as a child who just needed care. In a variety of other responses, some teachers (5 %) considered Jamila to be a hyperactive child, 4 % believed that she was careless, 3 % perceived her as having a problem of some type, and 3 % indicated that she was lonely. A few responses were grouped as "others" (e.g., suffering from poverty, worried, in need of love) with 5 % explaining Jamila's behavior in these terms. In addition, 10 % of teachers indicated that they lacked the necessary knowledge to provide an opinion about Jamila's case, and 10 % of teachers did not respond at all.

4.2.10 Teachers' Perceptions of Inattention in Vignettes 3 and 4

Tables 4.8 and 4.10 present teachers' ratings for both Jamil and Jamila whose behavior showed symptoms of inattention. Teachers' ratings showed no considerable difference between Jamil and Jamila in relation to gender. Half of the participants (50 %) perceived the children's behavior to be moderately serious in both vignettes. Some teachers (63 %) believed that Jamil's behavior would moderately affect his ability to make friends, and 64 % of respondents believed that Jamila would also experience moderate difficulty in forming friendships. Furthermore,

49 % of participants considered that Jamil's behavior would moderately hinder his academic progress, and likewise, half of the respondents (50 %) believed that Jamila's academic progress would be hampered to a similar extent. Also, 74 % of teachers perceived Jamil's behavior as moderately common in Lebanese society, and 79 % also felt that the behavior of Jamila was moderately common in Lebanon. Many teachers (58 %) viewed themselves as moderately ready to deal with Jamil's behavior, and 59 % felt the same about coping with Jamila's behavior. Some teachers (42 %) considered that it would be moderately stressful to have Jamil in their classroom, and a similar proportion (46 %) believed the same about Jamila. In addition, 58 % of participants agreed that both Jamil and Jamila would require a great deal more attention than that needed by other students in the class. Half of the participants (50 %) felt themselves to be moderately ready to implement an effective behavior plan for Jamil, and a similar percentage of teachers (52 %) believed the same with regard to Jamila.

Teachers' ratings of inattention symptoms appeared to differ a little in relation to gender, and their perceptions of inattention were apparently not influenced by the fact that Jamil was a boy and Jamila was a girl.

4.3 In-Depth Overview of ADHD in Lebanon

Thematic analysis was used to analyze the responses of the teachers elicited in the two FGDs: these were transcribed and then coded. In the coding process, transcripts were read, and we developed codes for each passage, which reflected the meaning of the passage read both as it stood and in the context of the FGDs as a whole. The coding allowed us to identify major themes and subthemes, and then each related code was listed under the relevant theme. A matrix was formed in which each column represented a major theme under which related subthemes were listed.

4.3.1 Perceptions of ADHD in Lebanon

The majority of Lebanese teachers were aware of the most common type of ADHD, namely, hyperactivity. They believed that ADHD is found in children who cannot focus, continually play with anything at hand, and move around the classroom a great deal. For example, one teacher stated, "A student with ADHD, for example, can't focus for too long; he just plays with his books and pens. He is an extra hyper student." Another teacher provided the following illustration:

> I have this child who cuts his eraser and throws it at his friends. It is impossible to see him sitting still. I ask him to stand facing the wall to stop bothering his friends but once I turn my back, I see him rolling over the wall and playing with fliers.

Six teachers described children with ADHD as those who are aggressive and bully their friends. For example, one teacher described a student in her class as a child with ADHD because, "He hits his friends to seek attention. He shows aggression and carelessness to my comments." Another teacher added, "[He is] not only aggressive, but also annoying. An ADHD boy would bully his friends, hit them and act as if nothing happened in the classroom." Overall, most of the interviewed teachers indicated that they perceived ADHD to be a condition in which children are hyperactive and restless.

4.3.2 Incidence of ADHD in Boys and Girls

Ten teachers perceived ADHD as being more common in boys than girls. For example, one teacher stated, "We as teachers barely notice cases of ADHD in girls. ADHD is more common and dominant in boys because they are so hyper." Another teacher added, "I teach different grade levels and I always find ADHD in boys but not in girls at all. You see these boys always moving around and unable to focus."

4.3.2.1 "Hyper" Boys and "Tomboy" Girls

As it is clear by now, our interviewed teachers were aware of the fact that ADHD boys are known to exhibit the major trait of hyperactivity. Most of the teachers used the word "hyper" for hyperactivity in boys, and the majority of our participants believed that hyperactive behavior is dominant in boys. Teachers referred to different instances of hyperactivity to highlight this fact. For example, one of the teachers said:

> I have a student who is doing well academically but he is so hyper. You see this kid under the tables, jumping and running the classroom. When he has nothing to do, you see him playing with his glasses.

With regard to hyperactivity in girls, teachers believed that this type of behavior is found in only a few. Our interviewees labeled hyperactive girls with a commonly used word in Lebanese society, "Hasan Sabi," which is a synonym for "tomboy," and described these girls as acting and talking like boys. One of the teachers said:

> I have a girl in my classroom, she's a 'tomboy' and she's happy about it, especially when her friends call her with this name; she sits and talks like boys even. Most of the time I send her outside the classroom.

Another teacher stated, "Some girls have voices like boys as well. When we talk to them, they don't even listen."

4.3.2.2 Dreamer Girls and Unconfident Boys

Nine teachers reported that girls are quiet and docile most of the time. One teacher stated, "Girls are calm and sometimes dream [dream a lot]; we need as teachers to give them love. Even boys, when they are quiet, we know it's a sign of low self-confidence."

Furthermore, "living on another planet" is another term that one of the teachers used to describe an ADD girl. One of the teachers said, "Some girls, we don't hear their voices in class, it's like they live on another planet. I think they are shy because if you look at their grades, they are ok. I don't see any problem." Overall, 12 teachers perceived girls as dreamers, shy, and "living on another planet."

4.3.3 Factors Affecting Children with ADHD

Our interviewees suggested three major factors that they considered to be influential with respect to the characteristics and gender of children with ADHD.

4.3.3.1 Parental Effect: A Major Factor in Relation to ADHD Children

Twelve of our participants put all the blame on parents and considered ADHD to be a result of inadequate parental discipline and lack of knowledge about ADHD. For example, one of the teachers stated:

> Parents raise girls to be quiet, that's one. Two, they like boys to be hyper. Three, unfortunately ADHD is increasing - you know why? Parents raise and spoil their children in a way that they become careless, and irresponsible.

Another teacher added, "I have a student in Grade 5, a boy who is the youngest in his family. He came after four girls. His parents spoil him a lot so you see him (el ared ma hamelto) inattentive and hyper." In fact, 12 teachers believed that parental spoiling has a major effect on ADHD.

However, three teachers considered that strict parental discipline was leading to an increase in ADHD symptoms. For example, one of the teachers said, "Some parents are just the opposite, very strict, tough, and hit their children. Therefore these children become so hyper, move a lot to grab attention in the classroom." Another teacher commented, "During parents' meetings, some moms come and nag about their children being hyper and ask us to threaten them in class by referring to their dad's authority."

4.3.3.2 ADHD: A Genetic Disorder

Four teachers stated that ADHD is genetic. One teacher said, "Well, it's genetic for sure. I use to teach at a school where some students had oxygen deficit and this had an impact on their understanding and hyperactivity."

4.3.3.3 Food and Sugar Effects on Hyperactivity

Eight of our interviewees considered that diet and reducing sugar intake reduces hyperactivity in students. One teacher stated, "I believe that sugar makes these kids hyper and that's why we need a dietician in school that can provide a healthy diet for hyperactive students." Another teacher added, "Not only is a dietician needed, students should stop drinking Coca-Cola which is full of sugar and parents should help and watch their children's diet."

4.3.4 Current Practices Used by Teachers to Deal with Children with ADHD

Teachers' current practices with respect to children with ADHD in their classrooms varied, with some stating that they paid extra attention to students with ADHD or kept them busy. Only two teachers had worked on a behavioral plan to target undesirable ADHD behavior.

4.3.4.1 Extra Attention and Resultant Jealousy

Twelve teachers believed that ADHD children need extra attention. However, some teachers complained about the difficulty in fulfilling the requirements of the school program. For example, one teacher stated:

> Honestly, I sit beside the hyper kid. I try to focus on him as much as I can, but working with grade 5 and 6 is hard because the students' work is most of the time one on one. I cannot really manage between ADHD students and non-ADHD students. I try my best to sit beside ADHD kids and give them attention.

Overall, 12 out of 16 teachers believed that the children with ADHD need to be given more attention than other students in their classroom. Unfortunately, two teachers reported jealousy problems from students without ADHD when they saw that their teachers focused on those with the disorder. For example, one teacher reported a problem relating to a student who did not have ADHD and his parents, saying, "ADHD kids need care but other kids get jealous from our extra care and complain to their parents, so this is another problem. Parents come to school and report their kids' complaints." Another teacher added, "Parents think we are biased when we give hyperactive kids more attention, and even high-achieving children start to imitate their hyperactive friends to attract our attention."

4.3.4.2 Extra Work

Seven teachers mentioned that the best way to deal with students with ADHD is to keep them busy with extra work. One teacher explained that she gives them responsibilities:

> I give Farid, a hyper student in my classroom, some responsibilities like erasing the board, collecting the worksheets, reading... This way he releases his energy in something helpful and this raises in him some self-confidence.

Another teacher illustrated a method she adopted to keep Ahmad, a hyperactive boy in her class, busy, saying, "It's hard to control Ahmad's level of hyperactivity, that's why I ask him to color some drawings while I give his classmates a dictation exam. I just need to keep him busy."

In fact, the participants' focus was on keeping children with ADHD busy with anything, removing all pens, erasers, and books that these children enjoy playing with.

4.3.4.3 Behavioral Plan

Only two teachers used a behavioral plan to monitor the inappropriate behavior of children with ADHD and, thus, try to reduce it as much as they could. One teacher said:

> I can't ignore the hyperactive kids in my classroom because over the year their behavior becomes worse and this will have a negative impact on their friends in class. I put in a behavioral plan and monitor the behavior to see who is committed and who is not committed.

4.3.5 Unmet Needs and Obstacles

All our interviewees mentioned that their schools had never provided them with training in how to deal with children with ADHD, and in fact, schools did not even have special education services. The teachers reported some of the obstacles they faced, such as parents' negative attitudes toward school psychologists or special educators. For example, one teacher said, "[A] long time ago we had a psychologist at school but not anymore. Parents refused to collaborate [with this psychologist]."

Another obstacle teachers reported was their inability to address all students' needs, and almost all of them perceived that the efforts they made with students with ADHD were personal efforts with no guidance. One teacher stated, "We are not counselors but we try as much as we can, as teachers, to help, but our chances to succeed alone are slim, especially [since] the number of students is large. It's just a personal initiative." Therefore all teachers agreed about the fact that they needed help, support, and guidance in relation to children with ADHD, especially since their schools did not provide either training or special education services.

4.4 Summary of Findings of Research on Teachers' Knowledge and Perceptions of ADHD

It is important to explore the knowledge teachers have about ADHD and the misconceptions they hold in order to be able to provide them with the necessary help and appropriate training. As the results indicate, teachers responding to the KADDS questionnaire showed a higher degree of knowledge about the symptoms/diagnosis than about the treatment or general aspects (causes, nature, and outcomes) of ADHD, about which they held many misconceptions, especially about the causes of the disorder, its comorbidity with other disorders, and its outcomes.

Furthermore, our study aimed to explore teachers' expectations with regard to students' gender in relation to the ADHD subtypes. As the results show, teachers' ratings for Jamil and Jamila, the hyperactive children in vignettes 1 and 2, revealed no significant difference. Although some teachers were able to identify these students as hyperactive, others perceived them to be aggressive, spoiled, or in need of help and care. Similarly, teachers' ratings with regard to the inattentive behavior of Jamil and Jamila in vignettes 3 and 4 did not seem to differ in relation to gender. Also, although some teachers were able to identify these children as inattentive, others perceived them as quiet, as dreamers, as autistic, or in need of care.

Our interviewees did consider that students with ADHD differ according to gender. They highlighted the fact that hyperactivity is common in boys since they show high rates of externalizing behavior. In addition, they held the misconception that being quiet and dreamy are common and normal characteristics of girls. In this regard, teachers were not able to recognize the fact that sometimes being a dreamer or quiet are signs of the inattentive subtype of ADHD and should not be ignored.

It is clear that cultural factors cannot but influence teachers' perceptions of ADHD in both boys and girls in view of the fact that we live in a male-dominated society.

As for services and programs, no program to support students with ADHD seems to exist in Lebanese schools. What tends to happen is that teachers give extra work and attention to those students who they perceive to be hyperactive, but no other option seems to be available.

Chapter 5
Teachers' Understanding of ADHD, Their Conceptions and Misconceptions in Relation to the Gender of Students with ADHD, and Their Training Needs

5.1 Discussion of Teachers' Perceptions of Students with ADHD

The first aim of our study was to explore the perceptions that teachers have of students with ADHD. Consequently, this section discusses the results that were obtained in relation to the two research questions of the study and therefore addresses teachers' combined perceptions of ADHD and explores the influence of the gender of students with ADHD on teachers' capacity to identify the disorder and their perceptions of it. We also highlight the availability or absence of programs and services in Lebanon at this current time. Following this are our conclusions, recommendations, and implications as well as the limitations of the study.

5.1.1 Lebanese Teachers' Understanding of ADHD

Research question 1 of this study was as follows: What knowledge do Lebanese teachers in the elementary cycle have about ADHD?

The findings of the KADDS questionnaire reveal teachers' perceptions of ADHD in relation to three subscales: general knowledge, diagnosis/symptoms, and treatment. However, there was no common agreement on the concept of ADHD and many debates occurred during the FGDs.

H.M. Berri, A. Al-Hroub, *ADHD in Lebanese Schools*,
Springer Briefs in Psychology, DOI 10.1007/978-3-319-28700-3_5

5.1.2 Conceptions of Teachers' Responses to General Knowledge Subscale

Teachers' responses to the KADDS questionnaire differed depending on which subscale was under consideration. Findings of this study indicated that only 36 % of teachers provided correct answers to questions in this section which addressed the nature, causes, and outcomes of ADHD. Based on the findings, teachers (54 %) proved to be knowledgeable about the possibility of an adult being diagnosed with ADHD. The literature points out that as many as 50 % of children with ADHD will evidence symptoms of this disorder in adulthood (Barkley, 2005). A proportion of the teachers (43 %) were also quite aware that the prevalence of ADHD in males and females is not equivalent, and this concurs with the DSM-IV TR (American Psychiatric Association, 2000) which states that ADHD is more common in males than females. In fact, our FGDs also confirmed that the incidence of ADHD is more common in boys than girls. In addition, a majority of teachers (74 %) were aware that children with ADHD are more distinguishable from normal children in a classroom than in a free-play situation and that the majority of ADHD children evidence poor school performance at the elementary stage.

Teachers held many misconceptions and lacked knowledge about many of the items in this subscale. First, participants (64 %) were not aware that symptoms of ADHD vary across tasks and settings. They believed that a child with ADHD who is able to focus on video games or television for over an hour should also be able to sustain their attention for at least an hour during class or while doing homework. With regard to this, teachers need to be alert that children with ADHD work best on tasks they have chosen themselves and that they find interesting. As Kleynhans (2005) says, they attend automatically to things they enjoy but can have great difficulty in doing new things or less enjoyable tasks. Moreover, they need to be conscious of the fact that ADHD children find it very difficult to focus on repetitive tasks, such as homework and schoolwork.

Second, 42 % of teachers did not realize that ADHD is an inherited condition. However, the literature points out that the disorder is strongly hereditary (Kleynhans, 2005). Thus, having an adequate understanding that ADHD is strongly hereditary should facilitate teachers' communication with parents and ADHD children.

Third, just over half of teachers (56 %) believed that children with ADHD experience more problems in unfamiliar situations than they do in familiar ones. According to Badeleh (2013), children with ADHD will show fewer behavioral problems in unfamiliar surroundings than in ones which they are familiar. Teachers need to take this factor into consideration since it is common to find learners with ADHD exhibiting better behavior at the beginning of the school year when exposed to new teachers, classroom, and peers.

Fourth, a percentage of teachers (45 %) lacked knowledge about the long-term outcomes of ADHD. According to these teachers, children with ADHD are likely to outgrow their symptoms by puberty and then function normally in adulthood. However, as noted earlier, 50 % of children with ADHD will evidence symptoms of this disorder in adulthood (Barkley, 2005). This implies that the seriousness of this disorder is often overlooked during an individual's childhood years.

Fifth, a high percentage of teachers (65 %) were of the opinion that children with ADHD display an inflexible adherence to specific routines or rituals, and Barkley (2005) confirms that children with the disorder have difficulty in inhibiting and self-regulating their behavior.

Sixth, there seemed to be mistaken views about the influence of home situations on children with ADHD. Some teachers (41 %) thought that the symptoms of ADHD are often seen in children without the disorder who come from chaotic home environments. In this respect, it is very important for teachers to understand that psychosocial factors do not cause ADHD, but may lead to ADHD-like symptoms (Howe, 2010).

Seventh, about half of the participants in this study (54 %) realized that in very young children, the problem behavior of children with ADHD (e.g., hyperactivity, inattention) is distinctly different from age-appropriate behaviors of children without the condition. According to Legato (2011), ADHD-related symptoms can be seen as "behavioral immaturity," and it is difficult to distinguish ADHD symptoms until a child is at least 3 years old. Therefore, it is important for teachers to remember when making a referral that it is both the degree of the symptoms and their duration that will determine a diagnosis.

Eighth, 44 % of teachers believed that medical doctors are necessarily able to make a definitive diagnosis of ADHD. However, this is incorrect since there is no medical test that can confirm a diagnosis of ADHD (Kleynhans, 2005).

Ninth, almost half of teachers (49 %) were unaware of the fact that depression is more frequent in children with ADHD than in children without the disorder. As such, teachers did not realize and thus did not take into consideration that many conduct disorders can be associated with ADHD, such as aggression, depression, and anxiety (Pires, da Silva, & de Assis, 2013). In addition, ADD girls are a matter of concern. They are considered to be more at risk and of greater concern than boys as they are more likely to engage in emotional problems such as depression, anxiety, and loneliness (Maniadaki, Sonuga-Barke, & Kakouros, 2003). A study conducted in England by Groenewald, Emond, and Sayal (2009) has shown that ADHD in girls compared to the condition in boys is under-recognized and that unfortunately teachers have difficulty coping with girls with ADHD and poor knowledge of the disorder's subtypes.

Tenth, some teachers (39 %) believed that a diagnosis of ADHD makes a child eligible for placement in special education. However, in Lebanon, we are moving toward an inclusive education system in which teachers have the responsibility to respond to the diverse needs of their learners, including children with ADHD, and provide them with support (Kleynhans, 2005).

To address teachers' misconceptions and the gaps in their knowledge, we propose a number of recommendations. Lebanese teachers need to be aware that ADHD is strongly hereditary and psychosocial factors do not cause it, but may lead to ADHD-like symptoms. ADHD-related symptoms may just be signs of "behavioral immaturity," and it is difficult to distinguish whether these are actually symptoms of

ADHD until a child is at least 3 years of age. Therefore, teachers need to bear in mind when making a referral that it is both the degree of the symptoms and their duration that are the determining factors when reaching an accurate diagnosis. Teachers also need to take into consideration the fact that such conduct disorders as depression and anxiety can be associated with ADHD, especially in girls. Therefore, improving teachers' knowledge about ADHD, particularly with respect to inattention, could assist in tackling bias in relation to gender. In addition to the above, Lebanese teachers need to be conscious that children with ADHD prefer working on tasks they have selected themselves and on those that interest them and such children's behavior will be better if they are in an environment that is unfamiliar to them rather than one that they know well. As mentioned earlier, it is common to find learners with ADHD exhibiting better behavior at the beginning of the school year which is when they are likely to encounter new teachers, classroom, and peers. Furthermore, half of the children with ADHD will show signs of this disorder in adulthood, and so it is important that the seriousness of this disorder should not be overlooked during childhood.

5.1.3 Conceptions in Teachers' Responses to Diagnosis/ Symptoms Subscale

With respect to the diagnosis/symptoms subscale, the study's findings indicated that the Lebanese teachers were very knowledgeable about this area. Findings of this study indicated that 62 % of teachers responded correctly to the questions in this section that addressed various symptoms of ADHD and its diagnosis. The majority of teachers were able to recognize the main characteristics of ADHD, especially the two clusters of symptoms: hyperactivity and inattention and the fact that a child's symptoms must be present before the age of 7 in order for a diagnosis of to be made. In addition, teachers recognized that children with ADHD are frequently distracted by extraneous stimuli, observing these children to be very fidgety. Teachers were conscious of the fact that symptoms of ADHD have to be present in two or more settings before diagnosis can be made. Also, nearly 80 % of the teachers were aware that children with ADHD have problems in organizing tasks and activities. Apparently, teachers' high level of knowledge of ADHD symptoms is the result of their actual classroom experience of teaching students with the disorder. Students with the hyperactive behavior are easily identified by teachers since they are always moving around the classroom and/or, during free time, behave disruptively and are unable to concentrate on their tasks or classroom work.

Most teachers held a variety of misconceptions and lacked knowledge about many items in this subscale. First, 48 % of the teachers believed that ADHD children have an inflated sense of self-esteem and their own importance. However, according to Sciutto et al. (2004), the symptoms of ADHD often leave the child with low self-confidence, poor coping strategies, and an impaired sense of efficacy.

Second, findings of this study showed that around 40 % of the teachers confused symptoms of ADHD with those of a conduct disorder, for example, aggression. Half of the teachers believed that being physically cruel to other people is a symptom of ADHD and that children with the disorder often have a history of stealing or damaging other peoples' possessions. However, teachers need to recognize that physical cruelty, stealing, and damaging or destroying others' possessions are symptoms of conduct disorder, not of ADHD (DSM-IV TR, American Psychiatric Association, 2000). This confusion between the two disorders also arose in the FGDs where some teachers expressed false perceptions of ADHD and referred the student with the disorder using words that describe conduct disorder symptoms, such as "aggression" and "hitting." Our findings concur with those of Hong (2008), whose study aimed to understand the perspectives of teachers who taught children with ADHD. Hong's findings indicated that Korean teachers lack knowledge about ADHD and face problems in distinguishing ADHD from other disorders (Hong, 2008).

5.1.4 Conceptions in Teachers' Responses to Treatment Subscale

Based on the findings, 68 % of teachers revealed themselves to be knowledgeable about the fact that punishment is not the most effective treatment for tackling the symptoms of ADHD, and it was clear that they realized that it is not an appropriate strategy for changing behavior. Positive feedback and incentives should be used rather than punishment (Kovshoff et al., 2012). Sadly, interviewees in both FGDs reported that parents of hyperactive students still resort to hitting, punishing, and threatening their children, with the father acting as the authority figure. Lebanese parents' attitude toward their children with ADHD concur with those of the Korean parents whose discipline methods are harsh and who regard obedience as essential to maintaining family harmony and functioning (Oh, Park, Suk, Song, & Im, 2012). According to Oh et al. (2012), authoritarian parenting practices are associated with poor social adjustment skills and higher levels of anxiety and aggression in children. Consequently, inappropriate parental discipline has been suggested as one of the factors that could lead to a greater severity of the symptoms of ADHD (Howe, 2010). An affectionate parenting attitude is important in preventing behavioral problems in children with ADHD. Therefore, not only teachers but also parents need to be open to more educational strategies to cope with their children.

Teachers held many false assumptions and were not knowledgeable about many items in this subscale. Clearly, teachers' lack of knowledge about the causes of ADHD influenced their views about treatment. First, half of the participants (50 %) believed that ADHD is the result of ineffectual parenting skills. Similarly, interviewees in both FGDs believed that spoiling of the child by the parents was a probable cause of ADHD. These Lebanese teachers' beliefs also concurred with those reported in the literature. For example, 65 % of Turkish teachers held this belief (Nur & Kavakci, 2010), as did 53 % of Iranian teachers (Ghanizadeh, Bahredar, & Moeini, 2005). Thus, teachers need to be aware that parenting skills are factors that may have an impact on ADHD but certainly do not cause it. As mentioned previously, inappropriate parental discipline (being very harsh or very indulgent toward the child) has been suggested as one of the factors that could lead to a greater severity of the symptoms.

Second, nearly half of the teachers (47 %) lacked knowledge of the effect of antidepressant drugs in reducing symptoms of ADHD. Based on previous research, there are three types of medication used to treat ADHD symptoms: stimulants, antidepressants, and antihypertensive drugs (Barkley & Mash, 2006). Medication was strongly recommended for children with ADHD by 60 % of the teachers in Gregg's (2005) study findings.

Third, a widely accepted myth that has emerged recently is that one way of treating ADHD effectively is through special diets (Weyandt, Fulton, Schepman, Verdi, & Wilson, 2009). Interestingly, 58 % of the teachers believed this to be true and our interviewees held similar views and considered that an appropriate diet and reduced sugar intake would reduce hyperactivity in students. Teachers need to be aware that this is only a myth and that this form of treatment gives false hope of a quick cure and may actually delay effective treatments.

Fourth, teachers in this study (31 %) believed that individual psychotherapy is usually sufficient for the treatment of most children with ADHD. However, according to Krowski (2009), children with ADHD should be given treatment in all the domains in which they experience difficulties. Teachers play a major role in the implementation of the intervention programs for these children, and their knowledge about ADHD is a prerequisite for them to be able to make suitable referrals and provide correct information to assist in the diagnosis process.

Fifth, teachers in this study (41 %) thought that behavioral/psychological interventions for children with ADHD focus primarily on the child's problems with inattention. In fact, behavioral and psychological interventions focus on all symptoms of ADHD, not just inattention, and on the management of these symptoms (Morisoli & McLaughlin, 2006). Therefore, teachers should play an integral role in implementing these behavioral interventions, for example, using positive reinforcements to manage their classes.

Sixth, teachers (46 %) were under the impression that the use of stimulant medication leads to increased addiction in adulthood. However, according to Kleynhans (2005), there is little evidence in the literature that stimulant treatment of children with ADHD increases the risk of later substance abuse, a fact of which teachers need to be aware.

In fact, teachers need to be conscious that inappropriate parental discipline, such as overindulging the child and/or being excessively strict, does not actually cause ADHD but it may indeed lead to a greater severity of the symptoms.

5.1.5 Teachers' Abilities to Differentiate Between Boys and Girls with ADHD in Lebanon

Research question 2 in this study was: How does the gender of students with ADHD affect elementary teachers' perceptions of ADHD?

Analysis of the four vignettes revealed teachers' perceptions of both the hyperactivity and inattention subtypes of ADHD in Jamil and Jamila. In vignettes 1 and 2, the behavior of both children was perceived by Lebanese teachers to be extremely serious and stressful, severely hindering their academic progress, and thus they were seen as being in need of more attention than other students. For our participants, Jamil and Jamila's hyperactive behavior was rated as moderately common in Lebanese society and most teachers considered themselves moderately ready to implement an effective behavior plan. Teachers' ratings of hyperactivity did not seem to differ between the genders.

However, the literature notes that hyperactivity symptoms are perceived excessively in boys in specific. According to Maniadaki et al. (2003), boys' high rates of hyperactivity make it easier for teachers to identify them, while it is hard to identify girls with ADHD since in most societies it is expected that they will be quiet. Also, Coles, Slavec, Bernstein, and Baroni's (2012) findings revealed that boys with ADHD typically show high levels of hyperactivity and disruptiveness and other externalizing symptoms that are obvious to teachers. In fact, the majority of teachers interviewed in both FGDs held the same opinion as that of Maniadaki et al. (2003) and Coles et al. (2012), whose studies refer to the prevalence of "hyper" boys as opposed to the small number of girls they called "Hasan Sabi" or "tom girl," who acted like boys. The majority of our participants perceived that most girls they encountered were quiet. Thus, there was inconsistency between teachers' ratings of the vignettes and the thoughts they expressed during the FGDs.

5.1.6 Interpretation of Hyperactivity in Jamil and Jamila

Surprisingly, few teachers (20 %) were able to recognize that Jamil was a hyperactive boy and likewise only 27 % identified Jamila's behavior as hyperactive. Some teachers perceived their case to be one of ADHD without distinguishing the subtype. The most common interpretations of Jamil and Jamila's behavior basically fell into two categories, which involved either labelling the problem or referring to treatments for it. Teachers' most common labels for students were "aggressive," "careless," "spoiled," and "messy." The most common treatments that they thought were appropriate for these children were providing them with care, referring them to a psychologist since these children had psychological problems, and giving them love. Additionally, around 19 % of teachers either did not know how to interpret the children's behavior or did not respond.

In fact, few of the Lebanese teachers were able to recognize that Jamil and Jamila were hyperactive, and their false interpretations highlighted the fact that these teachers lacked knowledge about ADHD subtypes and thus were unable to use the correct procedures to identifying the disorder. Most probably, the teachers regarded Jamil and Jamila's behavior as moderately acceptable in the context of Lebanese culture. This may be an explanation for their inability to link these students' behavior to hyperactivity.

Teachers' ratings of vignettes 3 and 4 which tackled the inattentive subtype of ADHD did not significantly differ according to gender. The behavior of both Jamil and Jamila were perceived by Lebanese teachers as moderately serious and stressful and likely to hinder their academic progress to a moderate extent. For our participants this inattentive behavior was considered to be moderately common in Lebanese society and most teachers considered themselves as moderately ready to implement an effective behavior plan. Teachers' perceptions of inattentive behavior were apparently not affected by the gender of the children. However, the majority of interviewees in both FGDs held different opinions and believed that inattentive behavior is uncommon in boys and that it may be a sign of low self-confidence. Moreover, they held misconceptions about inattention in girls, describing them as dreamers and "living on another planet." Interviewees' opinions were aligned with Sciutto, Nolfi, and Bluhm's (2004) findings, which highlight the fact that girls with ADD tend to show low levels of hyperactivity and high levels of internalizing symptoms. This pattern of symptoms is less likely to disrupt the classroom and thus it is frequently overlooked by teachers. Therefore, our interviewees' misinterpretation of Jamila's case as a girl with ADD can be explained by the sociocultural expectations of society. In the Lebanese context, hyperactivity is commonly attributed to boys and quietness to girls. Lebanese teachers overlook these girls since they are not disruptive in the class. Accordingly, Lebanese teachers' understanding of ADHD is linked to hyperactivity that predominates in males.

5.1.7 Interpretation of Inattention in Jamil and Jamila

Only a surprisingly small percentage of teachers (17 %) were able to recognize that Jamil was an inattentive boy and a similarly low percentage (15 %) that Jamila has ADD. Some teachers realized that they were children with ADHD but did not refer to the subtype. The most common interpretations of Jamil and Jamila's inattention fell into two main categories: the teachers either assigned a label to the problem or referred to treatments for it. The labels most commonly applied by teachers to students were "autistic," "dreamers," "quiet," "lonely," "lazy," and "slow learner." The treatment most frequently mentioned by the teachers for Jamil and Jamila basically involved providing them with care and love. Additionally, around 15 % of teachers either did not know how to interpret the children's behavior or did not respond.

Clearly, few of the Lebanese teachers were able to identify Jamil and Jamila as children with ADD. In this regard, it is very important to point out that teachers' misidentification of inattention symptoms may lead to failure to refer the students who require support. Results of this study show out that the seriousness of this disorder was frequently overlooked by the majority of Lebanese teachers in this study who perceived that students exhibiting the inattention subtype of ADHD behavior are just in need of care and love.

5.2 Services for Students with ADHD; Training for Teachers of Students with ADHD

As the Lebanese teachers indicated, virtually no programs or services are provided that specially cater for students with ADHD. Interviewees in both FGDs stated that basically they provide personal help for such students without any assistance from a counselor or a specialist. The enhancement activities, according to our interviewees, include paying extra attention to these students, giving them additional work to keep them busy, and providing them with extra activities, with perhaps one or two teachers using a behavior plan to monitor these students' behavior. These strategies were used to keep the student occupied so as to avoid the class being disrupted, as discussed by many teachers in this study.

According to Morisoli and McLaughlin (2006), teachers' knowledge about behavioral interventions has a big impact on how students with ADHD are treated. Unfortunately, only two teachers briefly mentioned these interventions. Moreover, Brook, Watemberg, and Geva (2002) emphasize the importance of training in relation to teachers' knowledge of ADHD. The majority of our participants stated that their schools did not even have special education services and they themselves had not received any training about ADHD.

All schools in Lebanon, whether public or private, must follow a national curriculum mandated by the Ministry of Education and Higher Education (MEHE). The scope of special education in Lebanon is limited to students with disabilities only, as there is no mention of ADHD in either Lebanese law or the revised national curriculum. This explains why there was no reference made to the provision of services, programs, and training in this study—they simply do not exist. The only activity that was reported in this study was the personal efforts made by teachers and the extra attention and additional work they gave to students.

5.3 Conclusions

5.3.1 Lebanese Teachers' Vision of ADHD

Today, ADHD is characterized as a developmental and neurobiological condition defined by the presence of severe and pervasive symptoms of inattention, hyperactivity, and impulsiveness (Daley & Birchwood, 2010). In the Lebanese culture, the term "hyper" is widely used to characterize the whole concept of

ADHD. Lebanese teachers are aware of the external symptoms that are easily perceived in the classroom such as fidgeting, moving around, and playing with their belongings to exemplify students with ADHD. Thus, the term "hyper" is extensively used by teachers. Interestingly, the findings of this study highlight teachers' great confusion when labelling these students. Children with ADHD, particularly boys, were labelled as "hyper" and/or "aggressive," and girls were perceived as "dreamers," "quiet," and/or "autistic" by a majority of the teachers. Tackling the confusion among these disorders could be a starting point toward teachers' understanding of the disorder and working on a comprehensive Lebanese definition for ADHD.

From another perspective, teachers' misunderstanding of the concept of ADHD could be explained by the lack of qualified specialists to train them and the absence of any Lebanese policy to cater for students with ADHD. To underline this problem, 80 % of participants indicated that they had received no training related to ADHD in their schools.

5.3.2 Current Identification Procedures

With regard to identification and assessment, there is no identification procedure because of the absence of either an official or even a commonly accepted definition of ADHD. In addition, there is no official, standard identification procedure in schools. What usually happens, as reported by teachers, is that they themselves provide personal help to students with ADHD, by giving these students extra attention and providing them with additional work to keep them busy. Most of the teachers identified their students on the basis of their external behavior. However, all teachers in both FGDs specifically stated that there was no official identification procedure in place in their schools. Therefore, no behavioral interventions were applied and the services depended on teachers' personal efforts, not on a well-structured program. We can conclude that we are failing many students because of an inability to identify them and then provide them with the necessary support.

5.3.3 Culture, Parenting Style, and ADHD

Perhaps one of the major misconceptions that came to light in the study relates to parents' inappropriate discipline. According to the literature, issues relating to cultural differences are important because they depend to a great extent on the background culture of the family and affect teachers' perceptions of children with ADHD (AAP, 2011). In fact, the Lebanese teachers in our study believed that ADHD is a consequence of parental spoiling and/or harshness. As mentioned earlier in the literature, inappropriate parental discipline has been suggested as one of the factors that could lead to a greater severity of the symptoms. In this regard, not only teachers but also parents in Lebanese society need to be aware of the symptoms of ADHD, the causes, and the possible intervention methods they could adopt with their children. Therefore, instead of threatening children with ADHD with harsh discipline from the father or overindulging them, the creation of a positive learning environment could help Lebanese teachers, parents, and students with ADHD. One of the major findings was the way in which gender plays a role in the identification of students with ADHD in Lebanon. Almost all teachers in this study mentioned that there are more boys than girls with ADHD. Moreover, Lebanese society and Lebanese school practices view ADHD as a condition that mostly affects boys. According to the literature, this is not only a Lebanese problem, but throughout the world, boys are being referred disproportionally more frequently than girls (Sciutto et al., 2004). Coles et al. (2012) suggest that this difference in referral rates may be the result of gender differences in the expression of ADHD symptoms. The Lebanese teachers, as mentioned earlier, defined ADHD by using the word "hyper" and particularly characterized boys with ADHD as typically exhibiting high levels of hyperactivity and disruptiveness. However, the Lebanese teachers referred to girls with the ADD type as "dreamers" and "quiet." These girls are generally overlooked by teachers in the Lebanese context, a possible explanation for which may be the fact that Lebanon is a male-dominated society.

5.4 Implications and Recommendations for Practice, Planning, and Future Research on ADHD; Recommendation for Improving the Education of Children with ADHD

This section focuses on suggesting implications for practice, planning, and for further research.

5.4.1 Implications for Practice and Planning

Many teachers admitted that they need help with ADHD students and that, in particular, they perceived their chances of succeeding alone to be very small. A step forward would be to provide more workshops and seminars in order to make more teachers aware of the characteristics of students with ADHD and procedures for identifying such children. More importantly, we should base any changes on the research findings concerning teachers and students in Lebanon. We should also address the needs of students with ADHD as best as we can by endeavoring to understand the cultural differences that affect the identification of these children. Teachers are the most valuable source of information in the assessment process, and in order to make good referrals, they need to be knowledgeable about the assessment tool in order to make appropriate referrals of students with ADHD.

5.4.2 Implications for Further Research and Recommendations

In this study, we explored teachers' knowledge of ADHD in terms of general knowledge, symptoms/diagnosis, treatment, and their perceptions of ADHD in relation to students' gender. Perhaps future studies could tackle teachers' self-efficacy and willingness to become involved in efforts to support students with ADHD. Moreover, there were overlaps between teachers' understanding of the symptoms of ADHD (hyperactivity in particular) and those of conduct disorders, particularly aggression, and between those of ADD and autism. Future research could study the differences between these disorders. Also, we can start over and begin a new program for ADHD because there are no programs in the first place. Since this study aimed to clarify the current views and misconceptions about ADHD, future research studies could include more in-depth analysis of identification procedures. Further study is also needed to learn about ADHD from students' and parents' perspectives, in addition to those of other school stakeholders (e.g., counselors and principals). Furthermore, future studies could target other school levels, for example, middle and secondary schools.

Some of the teachers talked about the need for the Ministry of Education and Higher Education (MEHE) to provide a standard checklist for teachers to use for identifying student with ADHD. This was a recommendation made by some of the teachers. Thus, one recommendation for policy-makers and decision-makers in the MEHE is that they could organize workshops and seminars about ADHD so that teachers would have a broader view of ADHD in particular and would have a clearer idea of how to identify a boy or girl with the disorder. In addition, they would need to take the Lebanese culture into consideration and not solely rely on the child's attitude in the classroom and whether they were active or quiet. Awareness campaigns to educate parents could also be initiated because parents are seen as obstacles by some teachers.

Another recommendation would be to include counselors and principals in the study, as they are important school stakeholders. Counselors and diagnosticians use multiple criteria for assessing students who may have ADHD and do not just focus on the behavior the children exhibits. They can also teach teachers how to assess and identify students with the condition and work together to address students' needs. Therefore, it would be very beneficial to provide programs for counselors and have counseling rooms in every school to address all teachers' and students' needs.

5.4.3 Strengths and Limitations of the Study

The fact that this study included a large sample makes it representative. In addition, it was conducted in both private and public schools, using qualitative and quantitative methods (surveys and FGDs), and was the first to be carried out with Lebanese teachers in public schools and in the south of Lebanon.

Although there were very few limitations in this study, one limitation is that only two FGDs were conducted. Another limitation is that the study focused on only two areas in the south of Lebanon so it does not necessarily represent the perceptions of all Lebanese teachers about ADHD. Thus, it would be better to include teachers from more cities and towns.

Only when teachers are well informed about all aspects of ADHD will they be able to diagnose students with the condition, refer them for appropriate support, and ensure they receive the best possible education to meet their particular needs.

References

American Academy of Pediatrics. (2011). ADHD: Clinical practice guideline for the diagnosis, evaluation, and treatment of attention-deficit/hyperactivity disorder in children and adolescents. *Pediatrics, 18*, 1–18.

American Psychiatric Association. (2000). *Diagnostic and statistical manual of mental disorders: DSM-IVTR*. Washington, DC: American Psychiatric Association.

Badeleh, M. T. (2013). Attention deficit hyperactivity disorder and elementary teachers' awareness. *Journal of Medical Sciences, 13*, 829–833.

Barkley, R. (2005). *Attention-deficit hyperactivity disorder* (3rd ed.). New York: The Guilford Press.

Barkley, R., & Mash, E. (Eds.). (2006). *Treatment of childhood disorders* (3rd ed.). New York: Guilford Press.

Brook, U., Watemberg, N., & Geva, D. (2002). Attitude and knowledge of attention deficit hyperactivity disorder and learning disability among high school teachers. *Patient Education and Counseling, 40*, 247–252.

Coles, E. K., Slavec, J., Bernstein, M., & Baroni, E. (2012). Exploring the gender gap in referrals for children with ADHD and other disruptive behavior disorders. *Journal of Attention Disorders, 16*, 101–108.

Daley, D., & Birchwood, J. (2010). ADHD and academic performance: Why does ADHD impact on academic performance and what can be done to support ADHD children in the classroom?: ADHD and academic performance. *Child: Care, Health and Development, 36*, 455–464.

Ghanizadeh, A., Bahredar, M. J., & Moeini, S. R. (2005). Knowledge and attitudes towards attention deficit hyperactivity disorder among elementary school teachers. *Patient Education and Counseling, 63*, 84–88.

Gregg, S. (2005). Understanding and identifying children with ADHD. Retrieved from: http://www.ldonline.org/article/5974?theme=print

Groenewald, C., Emond, A., & Sayal, K. (2009). Recognition and referral of girls with attention deficit hyperactivity disorder: Case vignette study. *Child: Care, Health and Development, 35*, 767–772.

Hong, Y. (2008). Teachers' perceptions of young children with ADHD in Korea. *Early Child Development and Care, 178*, 399–414.

Howe, D. (2010). ADHD and its comorbidity: An example of gene-environment interaction and its implications for child and family social work. *Child and Family Social Work, 15*, 265–275.

Kleynhans, S. E. (2005). Primary school teachers' knowledge and misperceptions of attention deficit hyperactivity disorder. Unpublished Master's Thesis. University of Stellenbosch, Matieland, South Africa.

Kovshoff, H., Williams, S., Vrijens, M., Danckaerts, M., Thompson, M., Yardley, L., et al. (2012). The decisions regarding ADHD management (DRAMA) study: Uncertainties and complexities in assessment, diagnosis and treatment, from the clinician's point of view. *European Child & Adolescent Psychiatry, 21*, 87–99.

Krowski, K. F. (2009). *ADHD: Urban teachers' knowledge, beliefs and classroom practice*. University of Massachusetts. These and Dissertations. Retrieved from http://search.proquest.com/docview/305140059?accountid=8555

Legato, J. (2011). *Effects of teacher factors on expectations of students with ADHD*. DePaul University. Theses and Dissertations. Retrieved from: http://via.library.depaul.edu/etd/66

Maniadaki, K., Sonuga-Barke, E. J. S., & Kakouros, E. (2003). Trainee nursery teachers' perceptions of disruptive behaviour disorders: The effect of sex of child on judgments of typicality and severity. *Child: Care, Health and Development, 29*, 433–440.

Morisoli, K., & McLaughlin, T. F. (2006). Medication and school intervention for elementary students with attention deficit hyperactivity disorder. *International Journal of Special Education, 19*, 97–106.

Nur, N., & Kavakci, O. (2010). Elementary school teachers' knowledge and attitudes related to attention deficit hyperactivity disorder. *Journal of Society for Development in New Net Environment in B&H, 4*, 350–355.

Oh, W., Park, E. S., Suk, M. H., Song, D. H., & Im, Y. (2012). Parenting of children with ADHD in South Korea: The role of socio-emotional development of children with ADHD. *Journal of Clinical Nursing, 21*, 1932–1942.

Pires, T., da Silva, C. M. F. P., & de Assis, S. G. (2013). Association between family environment and attention deficit hyperactivity disorder in children–mothers' and teachers' views. *BMC Psychiatry, 13*, 624–633.

Sciutto, M. J., Nolfi, C. J., & Bluhm, C. (2004). Effects of child gender and symptom type on referrals for ADHD by elementary school teachers. *Journal of Emotional and Behavioral Disorders, 12*, 247–253.

Weyandt, L. L., Fulton, K. M., Schepman, S. B., Verdi, G. R., & Wilson, K. G. (2009). Assessment of teacher and school psychologist knowledge of attention deficit/hyperactivity disorder. *Psychology in the Schools, 46*, 951–961.

Appendix A

Demographics Questionnaire

1. *Gender*:
   ______ Female ______ Male
2. *School*:
   ______ Public ______Private
3. *Which grade level do you teach?*
   ______ Grade
4. *How long have you been teaching?*
   ______ years ______ months
5. *What is your highest level of education?*
   _____ BA_____ BS_____ MA_____ TD_____ Other (please specify: ______)
6. *Have you received previous training related to ADHD at school?*
   ______ Yes ______ No

Knowledge of Attention Deficit Disorders Scale (KADDS)

Please answer the following questions regarding attention deficit/hyperactivity disorders (ADHD). If you are unsure of an answer, respond Don't Know (DK). DO NOT GUESS.

True (T), False (F), or Don't Know (DK) (circle one):

1. T F DK Current research suggests that ADHD is largely the result of ineffective parenting skills.
2. T F DK Children with ADHD are frequently distracted by extraneous stimuli.
3. T F DK In order to be diagnosed with ADHD, the child's symptoms must have been present before age 7.

H.M. Berri, A. Al-Hroub, *ADHD in Lebanese Schools*,
Springer Briefs in Psychology, DOI 10.1007/978-3-319-28700-3

4. T F DK ADHD is more common in the first-degree biological relatives (i.e., mother, father) of children with ADHD than in the general population.
5. T F DK One symptom of children with ADHD is that they have been physically cruel to other people.
6. T F DK Antidepressant drugs have been effective in reducing symptoms for many children with ADHD.
7. T F DK Children with ADHD often fidget or squirm in their seats.
8. T F DK It is common for children with ADHD to have an inflated sense of self-esteem or their own importance.
9. T F DK It is possible for an adult to be diagnosed with ADHD.
10. T F DK Children with ADHD often have a history of stealing or destroying other people's things.
11. T F DK Current wisdom about ADHD suggests two clusters of symptoms: one of inattention and another consisting of hyperactivity/impulsiveness.
12. T F DK Symptoms of depression are found more frequently in children with ADHD than in non-ADHD children.
13. T F DK Individual psychotherapy is usually sufficient for the treatment of most children with ADHD.
14. T F DK Most children with ADHD "outgrow" their symptoms by the onset of puberty and subsequently function normally in adulthood.
15. T F DK In order to be diagnosed as ADHD, a child must exhibit relevant symptoms in two or more settings (e.g., home, school).
16. T F DK If a child with ADHD is able to demonstrate sustained attention to video games or TV for over an hour, that child is also able to sustain attention for at least an hour of class or homework.
17. T F DK Reducing dietary intake of sugar or food additives is generally effective in reducing the symptoms of ADHD.
18. T F DK A diagnosis of ADHD by itself makes a child eligible for placement in special education.
19. T F DK Children with ADHD often have difficulty organizing tasks and activities.
20. T F DK Children with ADHD generally experience more problems in novel situations than in familiar situations.
21. T F DK There are specific physical features which can be identified by medical doctors (e.g., pediatrician) in making a definitive diagnosis of ADHD.
22. T F DK In school-age children, the prevalence of ADHD in males and females is equivalent.
23. T F DK In very young children (less than 4 years old), the problem behaviors of children with ADHD (e.g., hyperactivity, inattention) are distinctly different from age-appropriate behaviors of non-ADHD children.
24. T F DK Children with ADHD are more distinguishable from normal children in a classroom setting than in a free-play situation.
25. T F DK The majority of children with ADHD evidence some degree of poor school performance in the elementary school years.

26. T F DK Symptoms of ADHD are often seen in non-ADHD children who come from inadequate and chaotic home environments.
27. T F DK Behavioral/psychological interventions for children with ADHD focus primarily on the child's problems with inattention.
28. T F DK Treatments for ADHD which focus primarily on punishment have been found to be the most effective in reducing the symptoms of ADHD.
29. T F DK Research has shown that prolonged use of stimulant medication leads to increased addiction (i.e., drug, alcohol) in adulthood.
30. T F DK Children with ADHD generally display an inflexible adherence to specific routines or ritual.

Vignette 1

Jamil is an 8-year-old boy. Jamil's teacher describes him as always moving around in the classroom, disrupting his friends instead of doing his work. His teacher says that Jamil tries to find a comment for everything she says and doesn't listen to her instructions despite her constant remarks. He starts work late on his assignment because he's always playing with his pens and anything else on his desk. When correcting the assignment, he shouts out answers randomly and interrupts his teacher. He constantly has excuses and requests to leave the classroom and go to the bathroom. During recess, Jamil and a group of boys run around the playground, bump into their classmates, and throw their sandwiches around. When punished, he shows carelessness and persists with his behavior and attitudes. According to his parents, Jamil never seems to focus on what they ask him to do, even if they repeat it more than once. "He often wants to grab attention by shouting and disturbing everyone at home" said his mom.

1. How serious is Jamil's behavior?
   1--2---------------------------------------3
   not at all moderately extremely

2. To what extent would Jamil's behavior affect his ability to make friends?
   1--2---------------------------------------3
   not at all moderately extremely

3. To what extent would Jamil's behavioral hinder his academic progress?
   1--2---------------------------------------3
   not at all moderately extremely

4. How much of Jamil's behavior is common in Lebanese culture?
   1--2---------------------------------------3
   not at all moderately extremely

5. How ready are you to deal with Jamil's behavior in your classroom?
   1--2---------------------------------------3
   not at all moderately extremely

6. How stressful would it be to have Jamil as a student?
   1--2---------------------------------------3
   not at all moderately extremely

7. Do you think that you need to provide Jamil with more attention than you give others?
   1--2---------------------------------------3
   not at all moderately extremely

8. How confident are you about implementing an effective behavior plan for Jamil?
   1--2---------------------------------------3
   not at all moderately extremely

9. In your opinion, what is Jamil's case?
   ____

Vignette 2

Jamila is an 8-year-old girl. Jamila's teacher describes her as always moving around in the classroom, disrupting her friends instead of doing her work. Her teacher says that Jamila tries to find a comment for everything she says and doesn't listen to her instructions, despite her constant remarks. She starts work late on her assignment because she's always playing with her pens and anything else on her desk. When correcting the assignment, she shouts out answers randomly and interrupts her teacher. She constantly has excuses and requests to leave the classroom and go to the bathroom. During recess, Jamila and a group of girls run around the playground, bump into their classmates, and throw their sandwiches. When punished, she shows carelessness and persists with her behavior and attitudes. According to her parents, Jamila never seems to focus on what they ask her to do, even if they repeat it more than once. "She often wants to grab attention by shouting and disturbing everyone at home" said her mom.

1. How serious is Jamila's behavior?
   1-------------------------------------2-------------------------------------3
   not at all moderately extremely

2. To what extent would Jamila's behavior affect her ability to make friends?
   1-------------------------------------2-------------------------------------3
   not at all moderately extremely

3. To what extent would Jamila's behavior hinder her academic progress?
   1-------------------------------------2-------------------------------------3
   not at all moderately extremely

4. How much of Jamila's behavior is common in Lebanese culture?
   1-------------------------------------2-------------------------------------3
   not at all moderately extremely

5. How ready are you to deal with Jamila's behavior in your classroom?
   1-------------------------------------2-------------------------------------3
   not at all moderately extremely

6. How stressful would it be to have Jamila as a student?
   1-------------------------------------2-------------------------------------3
   not at all moderately extremely

7. Do you think that you need to provide Jamila with more attention than you give others?
   1-------------------------------------2-------------------------------------3
   not at all moderately extremely

8. How confident are you about implementing an effective behavior plan for Jamila?
   1-------------------------------------2-------------------------------------3
   not at all moderately extremely

9. In your opinion, what is Jamila's case?
   ____

Vignette 3

Jamil is an 8-year-old boy. Jamil's teacher describes him as a daydreamer yet well-behaved student in the classroom. His academic competence is a bit below his grade level. His teacher says that Jamil chooses to sit at the back of the classroom beside the window and spends much of class time looking out the window. When asked to complete a written assignment, Jamil starts working attentively at first, but then he easily gets distracted by extraneous stimuli (like noises in the hall), and he seems not to listen when the teacher speaks directly to him. After repeated instructions from his teacher, Jamil goes back to work but this time is too confused to get started. He also has great difficulty switching from one task to another throughout the day, added his teacher. During recess, the teacher says that Jamil doesn't harm anyone; he sits on the bench, eats his sandwich, and plays with Sami everyday. According to his parents, Jamil is a quiet and calm son. They feel that they need to repeat themselves when explaining and helping him with his homework because he loses focus easily. "He often seems to be living in his own world" said his mom.

1. How serious is Jamil's behavior?
   1---2---3
   not at all moderately extremely

2. To what extent would Jamil's behavior affect his ability to make friends?
   1---2---3
   not at all moderately extremely

3. To what extent would Jamil's behavior hinder his academic progress?
   1---2---3
   not at all moderately extremely

4. How much of Jamil's behavior is common in Lebanese culture?
   1---2---3
   not at all moderately extremely

5. How ready are you to deal with Jamil's behavior in your classroom?
   1---2---3
   not at all moderately extremely

6. How stressful would it be to have Jamil as a student?
   1---2---3
   not at all moderately extremely

7. Do you think that you need to provide Jamil with more attention than you give others?
   1---2---3
   not at all moderately extremely

8. How confident are you about implementing an effective behavior plan for Jamil?
   1---2---3
   not at all moderately extremely

9. In your opinion, what is Jamil's case?

   ____

Vignette 4

Jamila is an 8-year-old girl. Jamila's teacher describes her as a daydreamer yet well-behaved student in the classroom. Her academic competence is a bit below her grade level. Her teacher says that Jamila chooses to sit at the back of the classroom beside the window and spends much of class time looking out the window. When asked to complete a written assignment, Jamila starts working attentively at first, but then she easily gets distracted by extraneous stimuli (like noises in the hall), and she seems not to listen when the teacher speaks directly to her. After repeated instructions from her teacher, Jamila goes back to work but this time is too confused to get started. She also has great difficulty switching from one task to another throughout the day, added her teacher. During recess, the teacher says that Jamila doesn't harm anyone; she sits on the bench, eats her sandwich, and plays with Lea everyday. According to her parents, Jamila is a quiet and calm daughter. They feel that they need to repeat themselves when explaining and helping her with her homework because she loses focus easily. "She often seems to be living in her own world" said her mom.

1. How serious is Jamila's behavior?
   1--------------------------------------2-------------------------------------3
   not at all moderately extremely

2. To what extent would Jamila's behavior affect her ability to make friends?
   1--------------------------------------2-------------------------------------3
   not at all moderately extremely

3. To what extent would Jamila's behavior hinder her academic progress?
   1--------------------------------------2-------------------------------------3
   not at all moderately extremely

4. How much of Jamila's behavior is common in Lebanese culture?
   1--------------------------------------2-------------------------------------3
   not at all moderately extremely

5. How ready are you to deal with Jamila's behavior in your classroom?
   1--------------------------------------2-------------------------------------3
   not at all moderately extremely

6. How stressful would it be to have Jamila as a student?
   1--------------------------------------2-------------------------------------3
   not at all moderately extremely

7. Do you think that you need to provide Jamila with more attention than you give others?
   1--------------------------------------2-------------------------------------3
   not at all moderately extremely

8. How confident are you about implementing an effective behavior plan for Jamila?
   1--------------------------------------2-------------------------------------3
   not at all moderately extremely

9. In your opinion, what is Jamila's case?

   ____

Appendix B

Protocol of Focus Group Discussion with Teachers

Location:______________ **Date**:_______________ **Time**:_______________
School: ________________ **Number of teachers**: ____________________
(5 min.) Introduction

1. *Greeting.*
   Hello everyone. I would like to thank you all for participating in this focus group session. My name is Hala Berri and I am a Master's student working on my thesis at the American University of Beirut. Our session will last 60 min. I would like to have an in-depth understanding of your knowledge about ADHD. Before I begin, I would like to share with you some ground rules:

   - Everyone should participate, raise concerns, or give opinion
   - Confidentiality of names/comments/responses
   - Respect opinions (no right or wrong) and free to say whatever you want
   - Speak one at a time and as clearly as possible
   - Stay with the group and please don't have side conversations

2. *Purpose of the Focus Group Discussion.*
   It is an opportunity to explore your current knowledge about ADHD in Lebanon and the gender of ADHD students and its implications for your perceptions of ADHD subtypes.

(50 min.) Discussion
Opening statement: In this focus group, we are going to discuss a number of things. Kindly provide your input for the following questions:

1. From your perspective, how would you define ADHD in the Lebanese context? What are the characteristics of student with ADHD in Lebanon?

H.M. Berri, A. Al-Hroub, *ADHD in Lebanese Schools*,
Springer Briefs in Psychology, DOI 10.1007/978-3-319-28700-3

Possible probes: What do you know about ADHD? What are the characteristics that you look for when identifying a student as ADHD? What sort of behavior do you expect students with ADHD to have?

2. Do you think there is any difference between the characteristics of boys and girls with ADHD?
   Possible probes: What are the unique characteristics, if any, that you are able to recognize in a girl with ADHD?
3. How do you identify students with ADHD in your class?
   Possible probes: What are the current practices in identifying students with ADHD in your class? For example, is there a type of protocol that you follow? Describe a student that you consider(ed) to have ADHD. Include his/her characteristics and what particularly stood out about him/her that led you to think she/he had ADHD.
4. Does your school provide special education services for students with ADHD? If yes, describe them.
5. What kind of training, if any, have you received that prepared you to work with students with ADHD?
   Possible probes: Does your school provide training?

(5 min.) Closing Comments

The researcher will provide a summary of the points discussed and will ask the participants for any final thoughts or comments.

Thank you for your time and input. You were very helpful.

Index

H.M. Berri, A. Al-Hroub, *ADHD in Lebanese Schools*,
Springer Briefs in Psychology, DOI 10.1007/978-3-319-28700-3

The manufacturer's authorised representative in the EU is Springer
Nature Customer Service Centre GmbH, Europaplatz 3, 69115 Heidelberg,
Germany. If you have any concerns regarding our products, please
contact ProductSafety@springernature.com

Printed and bound by CPI Group (UK) Ltd, Croydon, CR0 4YY
30/09/2026
02225575-0004